Positioning
YOURSELF

Positioning YOURSELF

To Receive Breakthrough from God

ROBERT KEENA

Permission Statement

CONTENTS

INTRODUCTION

Have you ever felt your walk with the Lord has peaks and valleys? Sometimes you are on the mountaintop, and life is good. But sometimes you are in a valley—you feel abandoned and discouraged. This book will guide you into a closer relationship with the Lord.

You will learn how to develop a personal and more intimate relationship that will change your life forever and equip you to keep your intimacy with the Lord. As you apply these principles, you will see breakthroughs in your life. I have taught and applied these principles in my life and in ministry for over thirty years.

Therefore, I encourage you not to procrastinate and wait any longer. Instead, dive right in and allow the Lord to change your life forever. If you apply the Lord's principles in his word, you will experience the breakthrough you need.

CHAPTER ONE

The Goodness of God

We live in two worlds, the natural and the spiritual, which are parallel. When something happens in the natural world, there is a similar happening in the spiritual world. This applies to the flesh versus the spirit, where we battle the temptation of desires contrary to God's Word and long to be free in Christ. In our lives, we are mainly influenced by our imaginations, circumstances, preconceived ideas, and senses, which affect our attitude and trust in God's Word.

We need to renew our minds to the fact that God has prepared a blessed life, hope, and a future for us in the natural and the spiritual. We must understand that all the good in our lives, no matter how small or insignificant it seems, comes from the Father who loves us. He cares about every aspect of our lives, and this alone is hard to comprehend fully. Nevertheless, we have a part to play in our lives, and the blessings are not automatic—they come from a relationship with the Father.

In James chapter 1, the Lord says that God freely gives us every excellent and perfect gift—raining down from the Father who created all things from heaven and who is the same and will not change. He only gives what will help us.

Through his will and Word, we have been reborn and become his children, setting us apart as his prized possession.

Good things come from above and not from below. It's like rain coming down, a mighty cascade of God's unmerited favor. We are not left to the hand of fate or the circumstances in our lives. We are in the hand of the Father, and by his hand we are blessed. The goodness of God is on the earth and is available to us to see, touch, and feel. As we go through life, we need to change our perspective. Instead of looking at the negative, corruption, and evil, we must begin to choose to see the good—the earth is full of the goodness of the Lord.

In the creation narrative in Genesis one, God created all of creation, and after the completion, he saw everything was good because he is good. So, within the design of the world, things go on, but there is good if we look for it.

God is good, and he wants us to enjoy his goodness. Everything we have, even the air we breathe, comes from our father, who gives generously. The worth of God is expressed in his gifts to us—his grace. Therefore, we celebrate Jesus, who has given us the greatest gift of all, the gift of eternal life. We can't let anyone lie to us, and we can't lie to ourselves. So don't let Satan or the world deceive you about God. God is a Father, yours, and mine in Jesus, and we are his cherished children. He loves us with everlasting love, and he can't get over us. He's committed to us unreservedly and eternally. He is faithful, and he is trustworthy. He is good in who he is and all that he does. God is good inherently and individually. He is good morally and has no flaws within him. He is perfect, he is whole, and he is righteous.

God intends to do good things for us and wants us to trust that we will have a promising future. God is always good, and he shows himself to us on a personal level, no matter what we have done or not done, because he never changes, and his goodness is part of his character. Therefore, when his goodness is bestowed on you, he protects, guides, directs, and provides in all seasons of life.

Scripture states in Matthew 7:11, "If we who are imperfect and sinful know how to give good and advantageous gifts and lovingly take care of our children, how much more ready is our heavenly Father to give us wonderful gifts" (author's paraphrase).

Psalm 34:8 says, "Taste, drink deeply, of the pleasures and goodness of God. We are blessed, fortunate, and prosperous when we take refuge or turn to God. In doing this, we receive the favor of God" (author's paraphrase).

Therefore, we must be united, loved, steadfast, and yielded to God in our intimate relationship with him. The Lord is not withholding any good, profitable, or beneficial thing from us. On the contrary, he rejoices and takes pleasure in blessing his children. The Father is good—not absent or abusive but loving. He allows blessings into our lives when they will help us. Our loving Father is not selfish, doesn't hold a grudge, and is not stingy. On the contrary, he is generous and extravagant in treating his children and understanding their past, present, and future. He cares about everything regarding our lives, including everything we have been through or are going through.

Remember that every good gift comes to us from God. He only does what will help us. Because God is good, he does not change and cannot change—it's impossible. God is immutable. Because God does not change, we are secure, protected, and kept safe. Hebrews 13:8 tells us that Jesus is the same yesterday, today, and forever. Everything in the world is changing except for God.

What would hinder you from fully believing in the Father's goodness in your life? Over many years of being a counselor to men and women, I have seen that many of us had fathers and mothers that broke promises, and things changed. I have also found that women who have been emotionally, verbally, or physically abused and had their trust violated, especially by males, have difficulty receiving from the Lord.

Trusting God is difficult for some women because God the Father is presented in Scripture from a male perspective. Subconsciously, this triggers memories that have been buried for years. When they become close and open their hearts to the Father, these feelings and thoughts begin to awaken, and the memories are too painful to deal with, so they keep the relationship with their heavenly Father superficial.

Men who grew up with an abusive or dominant father have difficulty receiving from the Lord because the dominant male that was or still is in their lives dominated their actions—belittling them and telling them how to feel, act, and think about things. Their ideas are always wrong or stupid. This abuse makes men's feelings surface as they start to form a relationship with their heavenly Father, seeing him as they see their natural father. They become angry, defensive, and standoffish in pursuing a relationship with the Lord. When these feelings arise, they only see another male authority figure telling them what they can and cannot do.

June Hunt, in her e-book *Verbal and Emotional Abuse: Victory Over Verbal and Emotional Abuse* (location 76) writes, "Emotional abuse is the unseen fallout of all other forms of abuse: physical, mental, verbal, sexual, and even spiritual abuse. People often minimize the importance of emotions. Emotional abuse strikes at the very core of who we are. Emotional abuse is any ongoing, negative behavior used to control or hurt another person."

Women and men need validation from their mothers and fathers. When this is not received, that's when they look for love in all the wrong places. Unfortunately, many intelligent, accomplished people stay in abusive relationships because they have a victim mentality and do not receive healthy validation from their parents. Jesus loves you. He has demonstrated his love for you and validated you by his death and resurrection, so you have been given the most incredible validation. This is the only assurance you need—and you have it from your heavenly Father.

If you do not have a father or mother in your life or have an unhealthy relationship with them, know that God will validate you as a man or woman. I have often been asked this question: why did my parents treat me like that? The main reason parents do what they do is because they are hurt and broken from their past. Hurt people hurt people!

But our heavenly Father is not hurt, broken, emotionally unstable, or abusive. His goodness has been described in the Scripture as abundant, significant, enduring, satisfying, and universal. God's goodness is shown in his kindness, but that is hard sometimes to accept because of past experiences. Your life may lack empathy from others. People tend to raise red flags when others show kindness to them—you know, wondering what the catch or angle is.

God is good to us and has given us everything we have. God is good to all and all he has made. In Genesis chapter 1, the Lord created and said it is good. His goodness was manifested in all creation and is at the center of the Christian faith. Everything the Father does is for our benefit. He has provided our salvation and did not withhold his only Son for our good. His goodness offers all life-sustaining provisions, even the air we breathe. Our daily goal should be to demonstrate to others the excellence of God.

God is Personal

God is a person, and he is personal with his children. He is self-conscious and has intelligence, feelings, and free will.

God is a transcendent being who resides within his children and the world he created, caring for and maintaining it as a loving Father. I want us to remember what we have in Christ, for when we think about it, we will thank him. We can start with forgiveness of all our sins, his grace, and mercy that endures forever. When was the last time we thanked him for his written Word? The Bible is God speaking directly to us. All the blessings we have—material, spiritual, physical, and in our families—are gifts from God's goodness.

One example of God's personality being revealed is in Exodus.

"God replied to Moses, 'I AM WHO I AM. Say this to the people of Israel: I AM has sent me to you'" (Exodus 3:14). So, the Father has a name. It is I AM. I believe he is saying to his children within his name, I AM whatever you need me to be. He covers all of life. So, we can see here that the Father has a name. He is the one that was before, is present, and is for eternity—he spoke intelligently with understanding to Moses, addressed Moses's concerns, and gave him an answer and a solution. He feels the hurt and struggles of his children, and he is sensitive to our cries and suffering, so he has emotions.

Saul of Tarsus, also known as Paul, had an encounter with the Lord while traveling the road to Damascus.

> Then Saul, still breathing threats and murder against the disciples of the Lord, went to the high priest and asked letters from him to the synagogues of Damascus, so that if he found any who were of the Way, whether men or women, he might bring them bound to Jerusalem. As he journeyed, he came near Damascus, and suddenly a light shone around him from heaven. Then he fell to the ground, and

heard a voice saying to him, "Saul, Saul, why are you persecuting Me?" And he said, "Who are You, Lord?" Then the Lord said, "I am Jesus, whom you are persecuting. It is hard for you to kick against the goads." So, he, trembling and astonished, said, "Lord, what do You want me to do?" Then the Lord said to him, "Arise and go into the city, and you will be told what you must do." (Acts 9:1–6 NKJV)

Several events are transpiring within this one event. First, Saul threatens and murders God's children, believing he is doing the work of the Lord. Then, on his way to Damascus, he encounters the Lord. I call this encounter a destiny moment. A destiny moment is a moment in time when an event takes place that is for your present and future. These moments may not be like Saul's experience, but the Father sends people into our lives for a particular moment that will contribute to our destiny.

Second, Jesus takes our problems and concerns personally. "Saul, Saul, why are you persecuting Me?" The Lord is saying that when you are hurting, oppressing, withholding, and causing confusion to one of his children, you're doing it to him.

Third, we have to recognize when a destiny moment is happening. Saul realized this moment or event was beyond anything he could control. But Saul was wise enough to receive what the Lord had for him no matter how this moment was presented. Let me explain what I mean. Sometimes you ask the Lord for something, and the Lord brings the provision or whatever it is you asked for, but not in the package you thought it should come in. I have done this many times when the Lord brought what I needed, and I missed it many times. Because I thought the intervention should be in a neat package, exactly how I wanted the Lord to bring it into my life. But I have found that it always comes differently than I would like.

Fourth, Saul accepted it as it was. He made this statement: "Lord, what do You want me to do?" and the Lord directed him to the first step in receiving what the Lord had for him. Have you asked your heavenly Father, "What you would have me do about my marriage, my finances, my career, my schooling, my car, my rent or mortgage, that horrible manager or coworker?" Sometimes we are blinded by our circumstances. Father, what would you have me do? Saul acted on the word of the Lord, and he received his sight. When you receive the word of the Lord, don't only hear the word or direction from the Lord—you need to act on it.

God is personally involved with your life, concerns, and thoughts. On a flight once, I was thinking and talking to God about not seeing—it seemed I didn't have any talent or creativity. I was sharing that other people were given more skill and creativity than I had experienced. I was not so much comparing and analyzing the difference between different people. God told me it was due to their calling—they recognized their talent and acted on it. So I asked him what had happened to me. He said that many of his children don't work on their God-given talent. I played sports, was always a starter, and was pretty good but never over the top. Have you ever felt this way? It may not be sports; it could be art or a musical instrument. As I was thinking about this, the Lord told me to look out the window, and we were flying over the Grand Canyon. He said, "See my talent and creativity?" I answered, "Yes, I see it, but you're God."

I knew this was a teaching moment for me. He said, "You are created in my image and likeness, and you also have the mind of Christ. So, you have been given the gifts, talents, and creativity needed to fulfill your destiny. The skills may be at different seasons and times." As I thought awhile on this lesson, I asked how I could activate these gifts and when I would know they were triggered. He told me that some skills had started years ago, but I was not ready to receive and act on them due to insecurity, lack of trust in his goodness, and knowing I was unprepared. But those gifts are still active and ready for use. So, he told me to ask him to show me what these gifts, talents, and skills are, so I can act on them. With these skills, there would be some studying and learning, and I would need to get out of my comfort zone. I would need to develop and practice what I have learned. Natural things accommodate the gift. So, I started to ask for directions and steps from God on how to manifest the skills and talents he has placed within me.

"Everything you pray for with the fullness of faith you will receive!" (Matthew 21:22 TPT).

Always remember, the talent is there. Don't buy into the lies of Satan, who will tell you, "See what you have done? You did this. Wow, you're talented! You built this. You are excellent." To prevent us from buying the lie, we need to rehearse that God has given us everything we have.

> Lord, how wonderful you are! You have stored up so many good things for us, like a treasure chest heaped up and spilling over with blessings—all for those who honor and worship you! Everybody knows what you can do for those who turn and hide themselves in you. (Psalm 31:19 TPT)

Goodness has been stored and prepared for us who revere and love God. However, God has things in reserve that we have not experienced yet. God has been good to you and me, but we haven't seen everything, for more goodness is coming into our lives. There is a reserve with a vast and boundless supply of God's goodness. Therefore, never doubt the goodness of God.

Throughout the following pages, you will see how the father provides for his children in different circumstances and from all walks of life. Your past doesn't matter, so don't let it dictate your future.

CHAPTER TWO

The Plan

Our heavenly Father had a plan for us before we were born. King David wrote, "You saw me before I was born. Every day of my life was recorded in your book. Every moment was laid out before a single day had passed" (Psalm 139:16).

Our purpose and plan are grafted into the master plan of God—we all have different plans for our individual lives. Your existence is tied to this plan, the meaning of your life. But the enemy is trying to discourage and oppress you into thinking your life doesn't matter. He is always trying to get you to rehearse your past failures and shortcomings.

Our Father has a plan for dealing with those thoughts the enemy tries to get us to rehearse.

> And now, dear brothers and sisters, one final thing. Fix your thoughts on what is true, and honorable, and right, and pure, and lovely, and admirable. Think about things that are excellent and worthy of praise. Keep putting into practice all you learned and received from me—everything you heard from me and saw me doing. Then the God of peace will be with you. (Philippians 4:8–9)

First, we need to realize God has a plan and purpose for us, and each of us is part of his master plan. "'For I know the plans I have for you,' says the LORD. 'They are plans for good and not for disaster, to give you a future and a hope'" (Jeremiah 29:11).

I don't know about you, but I had an assumption in certain situations that the plan for my life was top secret, and I wasn't privileged to know it. However, I learned over thirty years that if the goal is revealed later, the Lord wants my attention to seek after the development of our relationship. The Father is more concerned about you and your relationship with him than a quick fix for a problem. Have you ever thought about why Jesus came? He did not come to die for the faith, healing, finances, or the church—he came for people, God's children. We are what he came to redeem.

Even when you miss it or don't follow through on your father's instructions, he still loves you and provides. But there are natural consequences for our actions. He is not punishing you—these are just natural consequences. Let me show you an example. In the garden of Eden, when Adam and Eve both disobeyed the Lord and ate the fruit from the tree of the knowledge of good and evil, the Lord banished them from the garden—natural consequences. But even though they were not allowed to live in the garden and realized they were naked, the Lord made clothes for them to wear.

He believes in us and has our backs in the good and bad times, when we struggle and when we excel. He knows we can do whatever assignment or task he has given us because he is with us all the way. Besides, he has the master plan.

> For we are His workmanship [His own master work, a work of art], created in Christ Jesus [reborn from above—spiritually transformed, renewed, ready to be used] for

good works, which God prepared [for us] beforehand [taking paths which He set], so that we would walk in them [living the good life which He prearranged and made ready for us]. (Ephesians 2:10 AMP)

This verse tells us what happened before we were on the scene of our lives. God did not leave us to an angel to bring his plan to pass. Instead, he took it upon himself. We are God's handiwork, his workmanship. Then he tells us what this handiwork is: we were re-created in Christ Jesus. The more we give heaven, the more heaven has to work with in our lives. Our works don't stay on earth—they go to heaven and live with us through eternity. So, it does matter what we do on the earth. However, we know works do not save us. Jesus paid the price, and we are saved through grace by faith in Jesus's finished works.

God has works for us to complete before we arrive at those works. He has already planned specific works to be done through our hands—that work is done through our lives. God designed these works before us. How are they going to come to pass? By taking paths that he prepared ahead of time. We need to walk on these prepared paths because the works he has for us are on the paths. We are empowered to fulfill the results as we walk in the ways prepared for us. If we stray from these paths, we cannot achieve the works because they become out of reach.

The Lord is not talking about plans for this moment. He's not talking about yesterday, last week, or last year. He said this plan was before time began and has been precalculated. Before the measure of time ever existed, God preplanned for the greatness he has for every life. Meaning we are well planned for. Our parents may not have planned for us, but God's plan for our lives is entirely in place.

We have a responsibility, and it's a privilege to walk these paths the Lord has prepared. So why would we want to take an unprepared course? There is no preparation on those paths of our own forming. But there is a full provision in the course God has prepared for us.

If we allow him to lead and we follow his program, we will succeed in the plans for all seasons of our lives. However, we will face circumstances that hinder us from fulfilling the goal God has for us to accomplish. Always keep in mind that God is not the enemy! So, it is up to us to learn to cooperate with all he has prepared. These goals, plans, courses, and ways will not just jump into our lives—we have to learn to receive them. Faith and generosity flow in two directions, the directions of giving and receiving. Please don't say, "I have a hard time receiving when someone blesses me," because this will make it hard for you to receive what God has already prepared. If we allow this, there will be unfulfilled plans on the path God has ordained for us.

God is careful when dealing with our circumstances. He knows what is best, meaning he is more concerned about us as people and our development—emotionally, mentally, physically, financially, and spiritually—all areas of our lives. We are the number one priority in his eyes. Let me ask you a question. What is most important to God in this world? I asked the Lord that question. According to Scripture, Jesus did not die for the faith, the church, or healing of sickness. He died for people.

> God loved the people in the world so much that he gave his one and only Son to save them. As a result, everyone who believes in the Son will not die. Instead, they will live forever with God. (John 3:16 EASY)

SMART Goals

Many of you have heard the term SMART goals. If you work in corporate America, it is everywhere. SMART goals are about setting and achieving goals for your career, department, or staff. Well, your heavenly Father has set SMART goals for you. They have the answers to receiving all the Lord has for you in life.

You may have seen this before, the word Bible used as an acronym: Basic Instructions Before Leaving Earth. It tells us how to live, respond, think, love, marry, raise children, manage finances, and pursue health, emotional stability, spiritual growth, and all subjects that affect our daily lives.

Let's look at each of these SMART goals the Lord has set in place for us. The one caveat is that you need to follow the conditions to receive the full benefit of the SMART goals.

S—STUDY—to set, fix, and apply the mind attentively to examine a subject closely.

M—MEDITATE—to dwell or think on thoughts, to revolve any subject in the mind.

A—APPLY—to be applicable, to put to use.

R—RESIST—to stand against, oppose, and strive in resistance.

T—TRUST—to have confidence, to strengthen, to have comfort, to be committed.

(Definitions taken from *The Dictionary of the English Language*, Noah Webster, 1828.)

Study

> Study and do your best to present yourself to God approved, a workman [tested by trial] who has no reason to be ashamed, accurately handling and skillfully teaching the word of truth. (2 Timothy 2:15 AMP)

Part of the plan is for us to study the Word of God. We can only get to know people by spending time with them. So, when we study the Bible, we spend time with Father God and learn how he thinks, acts, handles circumstances, and loves.

We place walls or guards on our emotions as a defensive mechanism to protect us from being hurt or having our trust violated. Studying is the activity that brings change, restoration, trust, confidence, and emotional healing. When we spend time with someone, we start to understand their ways, and once we know them, we begin feeling safe enough to let the walls down, and it's okay to let them down slowly and cautiously. Our Father knows our hurt that caused these defensive walls. That is why he is gentle and caring and deals with each of us in a way we can handle. He moves slowly and gently.

Studying the Word of God will give us strength and strategies for facing any circumstances. When I was 48 years old, I was in the TV studio filming our weekly broadcast. About ten minutes before the end of the program, I started having a heart attack. I completed the broadcast, and then my family called 911. When the ambulance arrived, I walked out to meet the paramedics. They saw me and asked if I was having a heart attack. Of course, they checked me out, and I was having a heart attack, so I was rushed to the hospital. During this whole event, the Lord kept speaking to me—not audibly, but a voice inside saying, "I have your back, I will not leave you nor forsake you, I am upholding you, and we will get through this."

The Father's words strengthened me and encouraged me to stand firm on his promises. When I was in the ICU, he spoke to me and said, "This is not the end, and you will not die." The Lord arranged for one of the top cardiologists in the nation to be on duty, who said he would handle my case. The nurses told me he was never on duty, but my Father made it happen for me. I have pulled through just fine and am active and living.

You may ask, how do we study the Bible? There are many ways to study the Bible.

1. You can learn by doing a daily devotional. I use Proverbs as a daily devotional. I read a Proverb and meditate on it all day. The book of Proverbs is a book for wisdom in skillful living that is applicable today.
2. You can do a topical study by using a concordance to show you all the Scriptures for your topic, like love, and you can follow it throughout the Bible from Genesis to Revelation. I would highly recommend you purchase a *Strong's Concordance*.
3. You can study biblical characters or complete books.
4. There are many resources online, like commentaries.

Meditate

> Study this Book of Instruction continually. Meditate on it day and night so you will be sure to obey everything written in it. Only then will you prosper and succeed in all you do. (Joshua 1:8)

We need to think about the Word of God we have been studying. When the Scripture states "meditating day and night," it means keeping the Word we have been studying in the forefront of our minds. The Lord knows we can't only think about the Word—he knows we must think about other things in life, work, and make decisions. So, he is saying to keep his Word in our thought lives.

When we meditate on something, it becomes a part of us, and it becomes a guide for our thoughts and decisions. Circumstances arise daily in one form or another—the Word will rise in our thoughts regarding how to respond to each case. Something will spew out when pressure is put on us— either the God-given strategy or the devil's defeat—it is our choice how we respond. The Word will produce results when we meditate on it, and our lives will flourish. We will receive favor, blessings, and provision and grow strong physically, emotionally, mentally, and spiritually. In addition, meditating on the Word will bring consistency to our lives, no matter the situation.

> He is happy when he obeys the Law of the Lord. He thinks about God's Law during the day and at night. He will become like a tree that grows beside streams of water. It gives its fruit at the right season. Its leaves do not fall off. Everything that person does will have a good result. (Psalm 1:2–3 EASY)

> His passion is to remain true to the Word of "I AM," meditating day and night on the true revelation of light. He will be standing firm like a flourishing tree planted by God's design, deeply rooted by the brooks of bliss, bearing fruit in every season of life. He is never dry, never fainting, ever blessed, ever prosperous. (Psalm 1:2–3 TPT)

Apply

> But don't just listen to God's word. You must do what it says. Otherwise, you are only fooling yourselves. For if you listen to the word and don't obey, it is like glancing at your face in a mirror. You see yourself, walk away, and forget what you look like. But if you look carefully into the perfect law that sets you free, and if you do what it says and don't forget what you heard, then God will bless you for doing it. (James 1:22–25)

We all have strongholds of some form, and many people deal with feelings of unworthiness, low self-esteem, pride, addictions, and many different vices. Or it could be abandonment from verbal and physical abuse that has created defenses. But to be truly free, we need to apply the Word of God to our lives and not just read it. The Lord gave us his Word so we can be transformed and not just informed.

"For if you embrace the truth, it will release true freedom into your lives" (John 8:32 TPT).

"Everyone who hears my teaching and applies it to his life can be compared to a wise man who built his house on an unshakable foundation" (Matthew 7:24 TPT).

We can see by the above Scriptures that applying God's Word is vitally important to our lives. When we use the Word in our daily lives, God's blessing starts to manifest in our lives, and we will experience breakthroughs.

Resist

> So then, surrender to God. Stand up to the devil and resist him and he will flee in

> agony. Move your heart closer and closer to God, and he will come even closer to you. But make sure you cleanse your life, you sinners, and keep your heart pure and stop doubting. (James 4:7–8 TPT)

To resist means to withstand, strive against, or oppose, to refrain or abstain from, to make a stand, or make efforts in opposition. Resistance can be a defensive maneuver on our part, such as fighting the temptation to sin. Resisting the devil must be accompanied by submitting to God.

The Father has given us equipment to help us resist when the enemy brings up our past and our failures or abuses. Telling us that we will fail—we won't receive the promotion or position, pass the test, or be accepted among our peers. We have armor to stand. As the apostle Paul said, when you have done all, to stand. Just stand!

The armor is an analogy in Scripture. When Paul wrote this letter, he was in prison, chained to a Roman soldier. He observed their armor and saw a parallel between them preparing to battle a natural enemy and the child of God preparing to fight against the devil.

> Be united with the Lord, so that you are strong. Then his great power will help you. Use all the help that God gives to us. Then you can be like a soldier who fights against the Devil. You must put on the whole armor that God gives to us. The Devil attacks us in clever ways, and we need to be strong. We are not fighting against human enemies. Instead, we are fighting against the rulers and the powerful spirits that have authority over this dark world. We are fighting against the bad spirits who live in the heavens.

Because of that, take all the help that God gives, like it is your armor. Then, when the bad time comes, you will be able to stand strongly. You will not fall. After you have finished everything, you will still be standing strongly in your place.

So you must stand strongly. This is God's armor that you must wear: God's true message will be like a belt that you tie round your body. Always do what is right. That will be like a metal shirt that you wear to keep your body safe. Be prepared to tell people the good news about peace with God. That will be like shoes on your feet. As well as all that, have faith to trust God. That will be like a shield that you hold in front of you. It will stop the Devil from hurting you with his arrows that burn with fire. Remember that God has saved you from your sins. That will be like a strong hat that keeps your head safe. Also, use God's message to help you. That will be like a sword that God's Spirit puts in your hand.

As you stand strongly like that, always pray for God's help. Pray about everything as God's Spirit helps you to pray. For this purpose, watch carefully all the time. Also, continue to pray for all God's people everywhere. (Ephesians 6:10–18 EASY)

The Lord does not intend for us to face our financial, physical, emotional, and family problems with our own understanding or in our own strength. However, the same power in Jesus is working in us right now! This power, when applied, makes us overcome and obtain breakthrough.

Trust

> Trust in the Lord completely, and do not
> rely on your own opinions. With all your
> heart rely on him to guide you, and he
> will lead you in every decision you make.
> Become intimate with him in whatever you
> do, and he will lead you wherever you go.
> (Proverbs 3:5–6 TPT)

The word "trust" implies confidence. It is a concept associated with firmness or something solid or secure. According to *The Hebrew-Greek Study Bible*, we can trust the Lord because we have confidence in him.

If we have given the Lord complete authority over our lives, we will not depend on our opinions or understanding. When we have allowed him into our lives, we will trust in him for everything and not try to figure things out or make things work on our own. The first thing in trusting the Lord is to accept the gift of salvation purchased by the blood of Jesus on the cross. Trust is immense—you trust him with your destiny, including your present, future, and eternity. When you live a life surrendered to God, you give him permission to lead and guide you in all the affairs of life. Allow the Lord to continue to build your faith.

Let's sum it up:

- When you study, it gives you understanding and the knowledge to work within the plan of God.
- Meditating on the Word transforms you from the inside out—changing, healing, and revealing the true you God has created.
- Applying the Word is when you show your faith and trust in God and stand up to your strongholds

and circumstances with the promises from God's Word that have taken root in your heart.

- When you resist, you stop allowing the devil to keep reminding you of your past and failures. You bring your thoughts under the subjection of Jesus.
- When trusting, you have done all to stand. You continue to stand because you trust the Father with your life and whatever circumstances you may face.

When we understand that God's supply, provision, and preparation for our lives is complete and lacks nothing, there is no room for worry or concern about our lives. If we know this, we can have the assurance that every moment and circumstance of our lives has a prepared response. If we live mindful that everything, we will ever need is wholly ready and waiting for our faith to lay hold of, that is how we live the good life designed for us.

CHAPTER THREE

Faith

> Now faith is the assurance (title deed, confirmation) of things hoped for (divinely guaranteed), and the evidence of things not seen [the conviction of their reality—faith comprehends as fact what cannot be experienced by the physical senses]. For by this [kind of] faith the men of old gained [divine] approval. (Hebrews 11:1–2 AMP)

Now (present time), faith is available, this means we can use our faith anytime we want to. Faith is always available for whatever we need, and when we don't see the results immediately, we can rest assured the Lord has answered our request.

What is faith?

God and his promises are the objects of faith. Faith is complete trust, confidence, and assurance—a strong belief in God and his Word. Faith in God is not leaping blindly without knowing who God is and what his Word says. Faith is simply trusting in God.

Why should we have faith?

> But without faith it is impossible to [walk with God and] please Him, for whoever comes [near] to God must [necessarily] believe that God exists and that He rewards those who [earnestly and diligently] seek Him. (Hebrews 11:6 AMP)

The Lord's Word tells us that if we want to please him, we need to have faith in him. In Ephesians 2:8, the Scripture tells us that we have been justified by the finished work of Jesus, which includes his death on the cross, his burial and resurrection, and his ascension into heaven. The Lord tells us four times that we should walk by faith.

"But the just shall live by his faith" (Habakkuk 2:4 NKJV).

"For in it the righteousness of God is revealed from faith to faith; as it is written, 'The just shall live by faith'" (Romans 1:17 NKJV).

"Now the just shall live by faith; But if anyone draws back, My soul has no pleasure in him" (Hebrews 10:38 NKJV).

"But that no one is justified by the law in the sight of God is evident, for 'the just shall live by faith'" (Galatians 3:11 NKJV).

For the Lord to tell us four times to live by faith, trust, confidence, and assurance, it must be pertinent to our lives. So, what does it mean to live by faith?

Just: guided by truth, in keeping with the truth.

Live: to experience or enjoy life to the full.

Trust needs to be based on the finished work of Jesus and who God is as revealed in his Word. When we understand and believe in his Word, this will result in us receiving faith because we know he keeps his promises. Belief also encapsulates hope and expectation.

"Surely there is a future [and a reward], And your hope and expectation will not be cut off" (Proverbs 23:18 AMP).

Do you remember when you were young, and your birthday or Christmas was approaching? Do you remember how excited you were and full of expectation regarding what gifts you would receive—toys, games, maybe a bike? There was a lot of anxiousness. Yet these events came with assurance and confidence; so does faith. When you live and walk by faith, you expect to receive from the Lord what you have asked of him.

"Ask me anything in my name, and I will do it for you!" (John 14:14 TPT).

Hope gives faith something to do. Faith requires action. We must act on what we have confidence and believe in, like God's Word. Faith supports and strengthens our hope. Faith and hope are the power twins for our lives. We ask in hope, and our faith brings it to fruition or manifestation in our lives. Our expectation is based on the hope that is in Christ.

"For we walk by faith, not by sight [living our lives in a manner consistent with our confident belief in God's promises]" (2 Corinthians 5:7 AMP).

"For we live by faith, not by what we see with our eyes" (2 Corinthians 5:7 TPT).

Walking by faith and not by sight—this verse describes the importance of getting free and not staying in our realm of living by what we see with our natural eyesight. Instead, it would help if we saw with our spiritual eyes. But, you may be thinking, how do we see with spiritual eyes? Faith is our spiritual eye. We know the source of the answer to prayer and the solutions to circumstances, even when we don't see them in the natural realm. God wants to bring us into the rhythm of living to where we are consistently experiencing provision in every area of our lives. He wants us to have a breakthrough in our thoughts, emotions, sight, hearing, and speech. Speech is critical when we are using our faith. We may have heard the expression "Faith speaks." Speaking is how God and Jesus operate by speaking his Word. Let's look at some examples. Genesis chapter 1 shows us this principle from the beginning.

In Genesis chapter 1, verses 3 through 31 state that God said, and his faith manifested what he spoke. These verses start with "And God said," and conclude with "And God saw." Words are containers that hold the power of your faith. You need to speak the Word of God to your circumstances over your children, marriage, career, travels, finances, physical body, and emotions.

Let's look at a war of words and the results. Are you familiar with the story of David and Goliath? David was a shepherd and eventually a great king. But he also was a liar, adulterer, and murderer. David made the hero's roll call in Hebrews 11, and God described him as a man after his own heart. The Bible does not hide David's sin—he committed and suffered the consequences of that sin. Yet due to his repentant nature, he experienced the forgiveness of God. David did not sin repeatedly. He learned from his failure. He understood and held on to his belief in the faithfulness and forgiveness of God. Your past has nothing to do with your present or future. God uses imperfect people.

> Goliath walked out toward David with his shield bearer ahead of him, sneering in contempt at this ruddy-faced boy. "Am I a dog," he roared at David, "that you come at me with a stick?" And he cursed David by the names of his gods. "Come over here, and I'll give your flesh to the birds and wild animals!" Goliath yelled.

David replied to the Philistine, "You come to me with sword, spear, and javelin, but I come to you in the name of the LORD of Heaven's Armies—the God of the armies of Israel, whom you have defied. Today the LORD will conquer you, and I will kill you and cut off your head. And then I will give the dead bodies of your men to the birds and wild animals, and the whole world will know that there is a God in Israel! And everyone assembled here will know that the LORD rescues his people, but not with sword and spear. This is the LORD's battle, and he will give you to us!"

As Goliath moved closer to attack, David quickly ran out to meet him. Reaching into his shepherd's bag and taking out a stone, he hurled it with his sling and hit the Philistine in the forehead. The stone sank in, and Goliath stumbled and fell face down on the ground.

So, David triumphed over the Philistine with only a sling and a stone, for he had no sword. Then David ran over and pulled Goliath's sword from its sheath. David used it to kill him and cut off his head.

When the Philistines saw that their champion was dead, they turned and ran. (1 Samuel 17:41–51)

In the above Scripture, we can see there is a dialogue going on between David and Goliath. There is a battle of words before any action. We need to speak to our giants and then act on our faith, trusting that the Lord has our backs. So don't look at the circumstances but at how great and mighty God is. Satan nearly defeated Israel because they chose to give in to fear instead of trusting the Lord. David had courage and experience trusting the Lord in circumstances beyond his natural abilities. David had the victory because he had a relationship with God. Connection is why you must spend time with God, reading and studying his Word, praying, and meditating on the Word.

Jesus used the fig tree to teach the disciples about applying their faith.

> Peter remembered and said to him, "Teacher, look! That's the fig tree you cursed. It's now all shriveled up and dead." Jesus replied, "Let the faith of God be in you! Listen to the truth I speak to you: Whoever says to this mountain with great faith and does not doubt, 'Mountain, be lifted up and thrown into the midst of the sea,' and believes that what he says will happen, it will be done. This is the reason I urge you to boldly believe for whatever you ask for in prayer—be convinced that you have received it and it will be yours." (Mark 11:21–24 TPT)

Throughout Scripture, we see how Jesus spoke to demons, sickness, and disease. Let's look at faith in action that brought provision to a sinking boat. God's Word brings more than enough.

> He got into one of the boats, which was Simon's, and asked him to put out a little distance from the shore. And He sat down and began teaching the crowds from the boat. When He had finished speaking, He said to Simon [Peter], "Put out into the deep water and lower your nets for a catch [of fish]." Simon replied, "Master, we worked hard all night [to the point of

exhaustion] and caught nothing [in our nets], but at Your word I will [do as you say and] lower the nets [again]." When they had done this, they caught a great number of fish, and their nets were [at the point of] breaking, so they signaled to their partners in the other boat to come and help them. And they came and filled both of the boats [with fish], so that they began to sink. (Luke 5:3–7 AMP)

A destiny moment is taking place for Peter and the other anglers. First, Jesus asked to use Peter's boat so that he could minister to the people. Keep in mind that Peter sowed a seed, his boat. Next, Jesus spoke a word of direction to Peter. Now, Peter had to decide: would he receive the word of Jesus and trust it, even though he was a professional fisherman by trade? Here is the destiny moment, a choice to go back out on the lake. Peter said, "but at Your word, I will [do as you say and] lower the nets [again]."

We can almost hear some hesitation in Peter's response. But Peter chose to act on the spoken word from the Lord, and when he did, he received provision. Prior to the word of the Lord, when Peter trusted himself and his knowledge, he received nothing. When we receive the word of the Lord, it may not make sense to our natural thinking. But faith is based on the truth of what we believe and not what we think.

I don't know if I have faith and if I could trust as Peter did by acting on the Word. Of course, everyone has faith, to what is our faith anchored. Jesus and his Word are the anchors for our faith, but everyone operates on different levels of trust.

Levels of Faith

As children of God, we operate on different levels of faith at various times and circumstances, so our faith will fluctuate. Don't let this bother you—even the disciples' faith fluctuated. But as you build and use your faith, it will stabilize and flow on a more even keel. Why do people operate on different levels of faith? Faith is like a muscle that must be worked daily, just like going to the gym and working out a particular muscle group. Faith must be used, and if we develop this muscle of faith, it will need nourishment. So how do we nourish our faith?

"So, faith comes from hearing, that is, hearing the Good News about Christ" (Romans 10:17).

Faith is strengthened and nourished by hearing, reading, studying, and teaching the Word of God. When building my trust, I would listen to teaching series and podcasts and still, today, I do topical studies. I read the New Testament from Matthew through Revelation multiple times.

> God has given me grace to speak a warning about pride. I would ask each of you to be emptied of self-promotion and not create a false image of your importance. Instead, honestly assess your worth by using your God-given faith as the standard of measurement, and then you will see your true value with an appropriate self-esteem. (Romans 12:3 TPT)

It's okay to have healthy self-esteem—some of you think too little of yourselves. For example, making statements like "I need to be more worthy" or "I have failed in the past, so I would not be able to do a good job." When we make confessions like these, it brings about doubt and anxiety.

Healthy self-esteem is based on who we are in Christ. This measure of faith in our lives is foundational and provided by God. We used it for salvation and the beginning of our trust in the Lord. This faith is available to all humanity.

I want you to know this: according to Romans 12:3 NKJV For I say, through the grace given to me, to everyone who is among you, not to think *of* himself more highly than he ought to think, but to think soberly, as God has dealt to each one a measure of faith. Every believer has been given a measure of the Godkind of faith, the same equal measure. Therefore, God has not given more faith to one person and less to another. Now it is up to you what you do with this measure of faith. Remember we spoke about how this earlier faith needs to be exercised or used. That measure is like a seed. When it is watered, it begins to grow.

Let's look at little faith and see what could cause someone to have little faith. When we talk about little faith, it does not mean the absence of faith, just a tiny deficiency that could be in one area of your life, not all.

> And if God cares so wonderfully for wildflowers that are here today and thrown into the fire tomorrow, he will certainly care for you. Why do you have so little faith? So don't worry about these things, saying, "What will we eat? What will we drink? What will we wear?" These things dominate the thoughts of unbelievers, but your heavenly Father already knows all your needs. (Matthew 6:30–32)

From the above text, we see that the worries or cares of this world can choke our faith to the point where we have little confidence and assurance in the Word and power of God to operate in our lives to bring the provision needed.

When this happens, we begin to take things into our own hands and try to make things happen. We need to remind ourselves that God is our source. When acting on faith, there are still natural things we need to do: take care of ourselves and our families, work, church, fellowship, and rest.

Jesus Calms the Storm

> Then Jesus got into the boat and started across the lake with his disciples. Suddenly, a fierce storm struck the lake, with waves breaking into the boat. But Jesus was sleeping. The disciples went and woke him up, shouting, "Lord, save us! We're going to drown!" Jesus responded, "Why are you afraid? You have so little faith!" Then he got up and rebuked the wind and waves, and suddenly there was a great calm. (Matthew 8:23–26)

In Mark's account of this Scripture, Jesus said, "Let's go to the other side." The disciples were given the spoken word of the Lord, directions on what to do, and God's perfect will. His spoken word is his perfect will.

Why did Jesus say to the disciples, "Why are you afraid?"

Jesus spoke this to them because they had decided to give in to fear and not trust the word of the Lord. They had just seen Jesus cast out demons and heal all who were sick with his words. They should have clung to God's spoken word and kept speaking forth the word that was said because it was his perfect will for them to go to the other side. It would be best if you kept talking about any storms or circumstances that arise as you move forward and act on the word of the Lord for your life. The enemy will put blocks and hindrances in your way to see if you will trip up and stop trusting the Lord and throw your hands up and say, "It must not be God's will" or "I missed it again." That is a lie from the enemy, and you must build your tenacity, so you won't be afraid to stand your ground.

We cannot control what we hear and see, and these things can hinder our faith. What we can control is not speaking doubt and fear when facing circumstances. Speak the solution, not the problem. Refusing to talk about fear will keep our hearts in tune with God and his Word. Too often, people sit around waiting and hoping that God or something else will make it happen. But by acting on your faith, you possess the blessings and promises of God. Something will happen once you have prayed, believed, and put action to the Word.

Look at faith in action in the book of Joshua chapter 6.

> But the LORD said to Joshua, "I have given you Jericho, its king, and all its strong warriors. You and your fighting men should march around the town once a day for six days. Seven priests will walk ahead of the Ark, each carrying a ram's horn. On the seventh day you are to march around the town seven times, with the priests blowing the horns. When you hear the priests give one long blast on the rams' horns, have all the people shout as loud as they can. Then the walls of the town will collapse, and the people can charge straight into the town."
>
> The seventh time around, as the priests sounded the long blast on their horns, Joshua commanded the people, "Shout! For the LORD has given you the town! Jericho and everything in it must be completely destroyed as an offering to the

LORD. Only Rahab the prostitute and the others in her house will be spared, for she protected our spies. Do not take any of the things set apart for destruction, or you yourselves will be completely destroyed, and you will bring trouble on the camp of Israel. Everything made from silver, gold, bronze, or iron is sacred to the LORD and must be brought into his treasury." When the people heard the sound of the rams' horns, they shouted as loud as they could. Suddenly, the walls of Jericho collapsed, and the Israelites charged straight into the town and captured it. (vv. 2–5, 16–20)

Think about being a part of this army following Joshua. What would you be thinking about the directions given to you to march around a city in silence? What kind of warfare is this? I could imagine there was talk about Joshua, saying he had missed it. What does he mean, to march in silence until he says shout, and these stone walls will come down? Sometimes you will receive direction from the Lord that intelligently makes no sense. But if we are willing and obedient, we will see the results. Sometimes we need to step out and trust the Lord.

I was asked to an influential woman's home because this woman could not eat and keep any food down, and her doctor planned to put her in the hospital. As we talked about God's goodness and all he has done, the word of the Lord came to me and told me to tell her that the Lord would heal her today. So, I did as the Lord instructed me. I told her I was going to pray for her, and the Lord was going to heal her, and she would eat a complete meal before I left. So as per the word of the Lord, I prayed and spoke healing over her body, that every organ and cell would perform a perfect work as

God designed it to work. Fifteen minutes later, she asked for a meal to be prepared because she was hungry. She ate the whole dinner, asked for seconds, and ate that meal also. She has been fine since and did not need to go to the hospital.

You have to put action to your faith. Sometimes we need to be bold and step out on the Word. In my natural mind, I was thinking, "What am I saying?" But I was fully persuaded in my heart that God would confirm his Word, and she would be healed.

"Then the LORD said to me, 'You have seen well, for I am [actively] watching over My word to fulfill it'" (Jeremiah 1:12 AMP).

As we act on the Word of God, he will confirm his Word that we speak to and over our circumstances, family, children, finances, careers, retirement, grandchildren, and school. So confess the Word of God in every area of your life.

According to Scripture, faith that takes the Lord at his word has been called great faith.

> When Jesus had entered Capernaum, a centurion came to him, asking for help. "Lord," he said, "my servant lies at home paralyzed, suffering terribly." Jesus said to him, "Shall I come and heal him?" The centurion replied, "Lord, I do not deserve to have you come under my roof. But just say the word, and my servant will be healed. For I myself am a man under authority, with soldiers under me. I tell this one, 'Go,' and he goes; and that one, 'Come,' and he comes. I say to my servant, 'Do this,' and he does it." When Jesus heard this, he was amazed and said to those following him, "Truly I tell you, I have not found anyone in Israel with such great faith." (Matthew 8:5–10 NIV)

The centurion took Jesus at his word. The centurion was fully persuaded that he just had to speak healing, and it would manifest in his servant's body. Great faith is unyielding—one does not give up until the request is granted. The centurion did not allow any obstacles to stand in his way. The Roman soldiers were very unpopular with the Jewish people. Don't let people, circumstances, or wrong mindsets stop you from believing and receiving from God. Don't limit God by expecting him to work only in a certain way or for certain people.

You may not know what it is like to be in a season where you feel like you are dying and still holding on to your faith. In a season where nothing is going your way, you keep holding on to your faith, trusting that God will do what he said he would do. But have you ever believed God would show up at a specific time or before a deadline, and he didn't show?

Have you ever told God, "I need you now," and it was like, "I will get to you as soon as possible"?

Jesus can get us out of any circumstances or trials we may be going through. He can give us the victory over it, and we can become stronger as we go through it with him leading the way. Know that he can get us out of every dead place we find ourselves in. Sometimes we find ourselves in the presence of Jesus and hear testimonies regarding someone's life. We can, at times, believe for someone else but have difficulty believing for our breakthrough in our own situation.

Sometimes we can lose sight of our faith. Sometimes we bury our faith or stop believing when circumstances happen, and we have no control over the outcome. Unfortunately, this is precisely what Mary and Martha, Lazarus's sisters, did when Jesus delayed in coming and Lazarus died.

In the gospel of John, chapter 11, the apostle tells us about the friends of Jesus whom he loved: Mary, Martha, and Lazarus. Here is a synopsis of the story's beginning.

Lazarus, one of Jesus Christ's closest friends, was sick. He lived in Bethany with his sisters, Mary, and Martha. So, the two sisters sent a message to Jesus, saying, "Lord, your dear friend is very sick." But when Jesus heard about it, he stated Lazarus's sickness would not end in death. Instead, Jesus knew he would do a great miracle for God's glory, so Jesus stayed where he was for the next two days. Then he said, "Our friend Lazarus is dead."

Consider the frustration of Mary and Martha as they were waiting for Jesus to arrive. They needed him now, but he didn't show up on their timetable. Then, finally, he showed up on his timetable. See, we ask, God responds by putting everything in his timing and order, and if we wait in faith, we receive the provision. At this point, Mary and Martha stopped believing, losing focus on who Jesus is: the resurrection and the life. After Jesus arrived at Bethany and saw Mary and Martha, here is where the story picks up.

> When Mary arrived and saw Jesus, she fell at his feet and said, "Lord, if only you had been here, my brother would not have died." When Jesus saw her weeping and saw the other people wailing with her, a deep anger welled up within him, and he was deeply troubled. "Where have you put him?" he asked them.
>
> They told him, "Lord, come and see." Then Jesus wept. The people who were standing nearby said, "See how much he loved him!" But some said, "This man healed a blind man. Couldn't he have kept Lazarus from dying?" Jesus was still angry as he arrived at the tomb, a cave with a stone rolled across its entrance. "Roll the stone aside," Jesus told them.

But Martha, the dead man's sister, protested, "Lord, he has been dead for four days. The smell will be terrible." Jesus responded, "Didn't I tell you that you would see God's glory if you believe?" So, they rolled the stone aside. Then Jesus looked up to heaven and said, "Father, thank you for hearing me. You always hear me, but I said it out loud for the sake of all these people standing here, so that they will believe you sent me."

Then Jesus shouted, "Lazarus, come out!" And the dead man came out, his hands and feet bound in graveclothes, his face wrapped in a headcloth. Jesus told them, "Unwrap him and let him go!" (John 11:32–44)

The Scripture tells us that deep anger rose inside Jesus. His anger was not toward Mary and Martha but anger at their unbelief. They were close friends of Jesus, had seen many acts of God, and should have trusted in who he was.

Jesus asked them this question, "Where have you put him?" Of course, the Lord never asks a question without knowing the answer. But he asked this so he could reveal something in their lives that he would address. Jesus wanted to see where they had buried Lazarus. What he was asking them was where did they bury their faith and beliefs, and where had they stopped believing his word? He didn't show up and ask the Holy Spirit where Lazarus was—he said to them, "Show me." God wanted them to own the responsibility for what it takes to see the provision of God's Word manifested in their lives. Show me where you stopped believing, buried the promises, and stopped having faith that I would come through in your situation.

Is our faith still centered around the great I AM? Is it wrapped around the fact that he is the way, the truth, and the life, or has it been displaced and misdirected? Have we allowed life circumstances to enter our belief and put our trust in a place that is not established and built on the rock, Jesus?

Once at the grave site, Jesus told them to roll the stone aside. Then Martha said he had been dead for four days, and the smell would be terrible. Once we bury our faith and stop trusting regarding the circumstance, we no longer want to deal with a stinky situation. We tell the Lord, "I wanted you to deal with this situation sooner, when I had hope, but now the marriage, the finances, the relationship, or career stinks." But Jesus said to roll the stone aside. We need to understand that God is not intimidated by the stinky circumstances we have buried. God will respond with his promises in his Word, but we must roll aside the stone of unbelief and start standing on his Word's promises.

Have you noticed that Jesus did not go into the grave once the stone was rolled aside? He said, "Didn't I tell you that you would see God's glory if you believed?" Jesus is the Word of God wrapped in flesh, and he is the Alpha and Omega, the beginning and the end, the author and finisher of your faith. In essence, he is saying, "I will restore all that the enemy has stolen from you, break generational curses, and heal the broken heart."

Jesus said to Lazarus, "Come out!" Here was a man that had not breathed for four days. Then, just by God's word, breath entered his lungs, and every organ began to function perfectly. So Lazarus, who was a dead thing, was brought back to life. Also, here was a man that was wrapped up and bound. He came forth to Jesus bound with the graveclothes. Many people think they need to set themselves free before coming to God, but the Lord said, "Come out, just the way you are." Have you ever heard this saying: "Could've, should've, would've, didn't"? The power to change is not within us—it's within the Word of God. So Jesus said, "Unwrap him and let him go."

"Jesus said to the people who believed in him, 'You are truly my disciples if you remain faithful to my teachings. And you will know the truth, and the truth will set you free'" (John 8:31–32).

CHAPTER FOUR

Provision

"And my God will meet all your needs according to the riches of his glory in Christ Jesus" (Philippians 4:19 NIV).

God's provision is always better than our limitations. We need to understand that we will always be limited in our abilities. But all things are possible to those who believe and trust God—God is not limited.

Because of whom God is and his character as described in Scripture, we can trust and rely on him to supply whatever we need in our lives. God always provides for his children, though it is often not how we expect or desire the provision will come. In the gospel of Luke, chapter 12 talks about the rich fool. There is nothing wrong with wealth. This person had more than enough, and he decided to tear down and build bigger to store more. The problem is that the provision is not within us but our relationship with the Lord. As the story goes, Jesus tells the man, "You're a fool. This night you will die. Who will get everything you worked and strived to obtain?" He had earthly wealth but no rich relationship with God. God gives us the ability to gain wealth, and this relationship brings wealth into our lives.

Provision is not just material or financial things, or even companionship. These are elements of provision. A provision is also a place—there is divine protection within this place. God doesn't permanently remove the peril in our lives, but he protects us while we are amid the threat. There is something we learn while under his protection in the middle of circumstances. We experience and gain knowledge of how to be patient, build faith and dependence on God, and cast, meaning throw off, all our cares or anxieties on him (1 Peter 5:7).

God told Abraham he would be a blessing to all families on the earth. Yet years came and went, with no sign of the blessing. So finally, with Abraham's natural mind, Abraham looked at the evidence of his age and the age of his wife, Sarah, and her barrenness. How many times have we known God told us about our blessings for the future, and we could not wrap our minds around it—we could not see, think, or imagine how this would happen? As a result, we even reason away what God spoke to us. But Abraham, with his "eye of faith," began to see the promises God made to him. God always reassures us about the blessings coming into our lives through natural things and words. For example, God reassured Abraham by the number of stars in the sky and the sand on the seashore. God protected Abraham from losing sight of the blessings to come, and the provision finally came into Abraham's and Sarah's lives.

The story of the widow and her two sons, which we will look at in this chapter, demonstrates this principle of protection. God protected her and her two sons from the creditor. He didn't remove the creditor—the Lord protected them until the provision manifested in their lives. So there is a process we need to embrace as we go through situations.

ROBERT KEENA

Worry vs. Trust in God

> That is why I tell you not to worry about
> everyday life—whether you have enough
> food and drink, or enough clothes to wear.
> Isn't life more than food, and your body
> more than clothing? Look at the birds.
> They don't plant or harvest or store food in
> barns, for your heavenly Father feeds them.
> And aren't you far more valuable to him
> than they are? Can all your worries add a
> single moment to your life?
>
> And why worry about your clothing?
> Look at the lilies of the field and how
> they grow. They don't work or make their
> clothing, yet Solomon in all his glory was
> not dressed as beautifully as they are. And
> if God cares so wonderfully for wildflowers
> that are here today and thrown into the fire
> tomorrow, he will certainly care for you.
> Why do you have so little faith?
>
> So, don't worry about these things,
> saying, "What will we eat? What will we
> drink? What will we wear?" These things
> dominate the thoughts of unbelievers, but
> your heavenly Father already knows all your
> needs. Seek the Kingdom of God above
> all else, and live righteously, and he will
> give you everything you need. (Matthew
> 6:25–33)

Worry is one of the hardest-hitting and heaviest
onslaughts the enemy uses against us. He bombards our
minds with real and imagined concerns daily, getting us
thinking about scenarios that haven't even happened. As we
resist worry in our thoughts, the enemy will try to draw us
back into the pattern of worry. Secret fears are interesting

things. Often, they can remain undetected until the actual resistance starts. Yet Jesus, in the above Scripture, assures us that our Father has faithfully provided for all our needs because he knows what we need, so there is no need for anxiety. Therefore, we must continually remind ourselves that God will provide and that the blessing is coming.

To seek the kingdom of God, we must first go to God.

Find the provision or promises in his Word that guarantee the outcome. Then, standing on his Word, resist with his Word in your heart and mind—speaking those words into your situation or circumstance. Jesus, when tempted, resisted with words, as recorded in the gospels of Matthew, Mark, and Luke.

The enemy's strategy is to draw us back to an old habit, and he does this as we resist and fight worry. He tries to work every angle, focusing on one thing, and then he brings something else from the past. In counseling sessions over the years, I have heard people tell me, "I thought I dealt with that stronghold or habit, but now that I am fighting this area, it has come back up in my thoughts." Remember, what we think about is how we will act. I shared this strategy on how to win this fight: stand in the power of God, resist thoughts in the name of Jesus, and allow the Holy Spirit to fill your thoughts with God's Word. A habit creates a space in our lives, and this void will need to be filled. Therefore, we fill it with God's Word.

If we don't give God first place in every area of our lives, like family, business, career, and material objects, we can place goals above our relationship with God. These things can become our God. We need to choose who or what will be our God. We must be careful about what we choose to be our God—making sure it can heal us, set us free from habits, and find our children if needed. On one of my missionary trips to South America, I was told a child was missing, so the pastor and I began praying that the Lord would lead the family to the child. In this country small children are taken, and their organs sold on the black market. Through prayer, the Lord led the parents and the police to the child's location, and they found her in a back room of a house. When we study the life of Jesus, we see that he was a man of great intensity of purpose. We must be people of intense purpose, focused on God's provision, plan, and direction.

If we stand against the trials and temptations of life, we must believe that God is a God of provision, even of miracles. We must have such confidence in the Lord that even the impossible circumstances of life will not discourage us and lead us into despair and hopelessness. We must be strong in our faith, knowing beyond a shadow of a doubt that God has a plan and provision of victory in all our life situations. So many people have faith in what Jesus could do when he was here on earth and what he will do in the future. But they forget and lose perspective on who he is now in the present day—the living Word.

A Widow's Provision

According to the Jewish historian Josephus, the widow in the story recorded in 2 Kings 4:1–7 was the wife of the prophet Obadiah, the palace administrator for King Ahab. Obadiah hid 100 prophets in two caves and fed them for an extended time during Jezebel's introduction of Baal worship in Israel. According to the Targum (an Aramaic paraphrase of the Hebrew Bible), Obadiah had borrowed money from Ahab to provide for these prophets.

This now-widow had been married to this prophet, a man who was a devout believer in the Lord. They had two sons, and she enjoyed time with her family. Unfortunately, events over time brought the family to insolvency, to the point of the creditor coming to take her sons and enslave them until the debt had been paid. Family members were considered assets to pay off debt during this historical period. According to Exodus 21:2, if someone bought a Hebrew servant, they would serve for six years, and in the seventh year (the year of Jubilee), they would be freed, owing nothing to the creditor.

Let us read her story:

> One day the widow of a member of the group of prophets came to Elisha and cried out, "My husband who served you is dead, and you know how he feared the LORD. But now a creditor has come, threatening to take my two sons as slaves." "What can I do to help you?" Elisha asked. "Tell me, what do you have in the house?"
>
> "Nothing at all, except a flask of olive oil," she replied. And Elisha said, "Borrow as many empty jars as you can from your friends and neighbors. Then go into your house with your sons and shut the door behind you. Pour olive oil from your flask into the jars, setting each one aside when it is filled." So, she did as she was told. Her sons kept bringing jars to her, and she filled one after another.
>
> Soon every container was full to the brim! "Bring me another jar," she said to one of her sons. "There aren't any more!" he told her. And then the olive oil stopped flowing. When she told the man of God what had happened, he said to her, "Now sell the olive oil and pay your debts, and you and your sons can live on what is left over." (2 Kings 4:1–7)

I can only imagine how she could have felt. Despair filled her and she couldn't sleep, being full of anxiety, wondering what would happen next. Now she is a single mom trying to provide for her family. Yet before reaching out to the prophet of God, she may have sold everything except the jar of oil, trying to pay the debt to the creditor. How often do we take things into our own hands before going to God for help?

Her husband and their father are gone, leaving them ill-prepared and experiencing emotional and financial hardship. At this time, she was living on promises she couldn't fulfill. But God already had a person to deliver his word that would usher in the needed provision, a miracle. The Lord sent Elisha. Now Elisha focused on the needs of the people wherever he was, demonstrating God's love and concern for their condition. He showed the people the heart of God and how much he cared for them. The Lord will send people into our lives with a heart for God and no personal agendas. We need to be sensitive to the leading of the Holy Spirit to recognize these people the Lord sends.

By the time Elisha steps onto the scene, this women's pockets are empty, the cabinets are bare, and she is down to losing her sons to the creditor. What kind of mother wants to give up her two sons to pay off a debt? So, we know this is not how she wanted her life to go, yet this is where her life was, and she was a woman of God. But trouble is no respecter of persons—it will come to anybody. Bad things happen to good people.

It doesn't matter how we pray, fast, or dance all over the house—this does not exempt us from dark days, empty days, or the winds of life. Unfortunately, we are seeing this woman's life not in the good times. The Bible didn't mention when the cabinets were full, the closets were overflowing, and there was money in the bank. Because that is irrelevant. God shows us how to survive in times of emptiness.

So, with Elisha on the scene, she reminds him of who her husband was. She states, "My husband was your mentee and attended your school of the prophets. He was a good man of God." This woman lived in a time when women were regarded as inferior, which leads us to conclude she didn't think she had the clout to approach Elisha in her own name. But she was in desperate need. Sometimes we must step out in faith and be bold to receive what we need from our heavenly Father.

Her Destiny Moment

Elisha said to her, "What can I do to help you?" Then he asked her what was in her house. What is significant about this question is that God will always use something we already have. For example, a jar of oil, a loaf of bread and two fish, or a donkey's jawbone. So, what we see or overlook as not valuable or not helpful in our hands becomes invaluable in God's hands. She was talking about what she didn't have; Elisha was going to reveal to her what she did have. The wisdom of God will always show us what we have, no matter how small or insignificant it may seem. God never uses what we've lost—he is not interested in a list of who hurt us or did wrong. See, he doesn't need anything we lost to bless us. Instead, he will use what we have left. Faith doesn't develop when we are on the mountaintop. It grows while we are in the valley when everything breaks loose in our lives.

The Process

When she received the word of the Lord, she didn't think the prophet missed it! She didn't say or think that it was not God's advice. She may not have yet understood how this would resolve her situation. After all, the creditor was on the way to take her sons. Nevertheless, she chose to accept the word of God and act on it. Sometimes we need help understanding the process or the outcome when the word of the Lord comes to us. Therefore, you will need to trust and be confident in the one who gave you the direction. Elisha told her to borrow. Sometimes, when you are broken, hurt, discouraged, or feel abandoned, it's hard to borrow what little energy you have to act on the word of God because the outcome is not known. Within this text, the Lord's word was to borrow from her neighbors, and not just some but many. When we are backed into a corner, we will find we have more strength than we thought. When we come to the place where if we don't believe in God's Word, we will lose the house, our business, and our loved ones—we're going down. The Lord's word was to borrow from her neighbors, and not just some but many empty jars. It would be best if we were empty and vulnerable to have a faith experience. When we have no other option, no contingency plan, and God has our undivided attention, that's when God will show up with the provision.

What is your capacity for receiving God's instructions and blessings? The number of jars collected is symbolic of her faith in receiving, and we can't receive above our faith level or capacity to receive. To expand our capacity, we need to be empty. The emptier we are of ourselves, the more we can receive. The John the Baptist said, "Jesus must become greater, but I must become less important" (John 3:30 EASY). When we are hungry and thirsty for God, God will fill us. How big can you dream?

The widow had to prepare to receive the blessing of God. The first part of the preparation was for her to believe and trust the Lord's word. Then she had to go and borrow vessels, so she would be prepared for the blessing.

"If you are willing and obedient, you will eat the good things of the land" (Isaiah 1:19 NIV).

Many times, in my life, I have been willing but not obedient, and then I would be obedient but not willing. Let me explain what I mean. There was a time when the Lord's word would come to me, and I would receive it, but I procrastinated and never got around to doing it. Many years ago, men of God spoke the word of the Lord to me about writing books. I was a young man and new in the ministry. I pastored several churches, had a weekly TV broadcast, and ministered on four continents, seeing many miracles and salvations. I am now writing books after thirty-plus years of ministry. Why did I procrastinate? I had insecurity and didn't feel adequate to write books. There have also been times when the Lord would instruct me to step out and trust him, but I was not willing. I did it out of obedience, but in my heart I was not willing and didn't like it. It is like telling a child to sit down, and they do it, but inside they are standing up. Applying what I'm sharing with you in this book, the Lord has set me free from my insecurity. A personal relationship with the Lord is a matter of the heart.

What is your capacity for receiving the instructions and blessings of the Lord for your life? When we find that the provision of the Lord has come to a halt, the need is usually fully supplied, or there is no more room to receive. Nevertheless, the blessing will sometimes flow into our lives for a while and then stop. Just like the children of Israel when they were in the wilderness for forty years after being set free from bondage in Egypt. The blessing of God kept them fed, and their shoes did not wear out. The Lord provided every day for forty years. When the blessing is sustained for a long time, we can quickly lose focus on the blesser and start focusing on the blessings.

What the widow did was to be done without distractions, in privacy, behind closed doors, so she and her sons could focus on the Lord and set their hearts upon him. Spending time alone with God is vital for any believer, especially today with all life's activities and busyness—school, after-school programs, sports, dance, and gymnastics, to name a few.

While meditating on this text, I concluded that this godly woman knew her capacity to receive and not allow greed to enter her and her sons' lives. Therefore, they gathered what they could collect according to their faith. The result was she received enough money to pay off the balance of her husband's debt to the creditor with enough left over to live on.

CHAPTER FIVE

Heart's Desire

We need to think about how we would be impacted if we received exactly everything we desired. For example, would this draw us closer to the Lord or away from him? Would it change our relationship with God? What motivates the desires of our hearts? Of course, we all have desires of our hearts, and nothing is wrong with that. However, can we ask God for the desires of our hearts? It will depend on what the request is.

Psalm 37:4 says, "Take delight in the LORD, and he will give you your heart's desires." Commit, giving God the right to direct and guide your life. Trust in him, and he will give us the desires of our hearts. We must give our heart's desire to God, so he can tweak our desire to align with his will. We are transferring our desire to him, so he can evaluate and change it in any way he wants. The heart is not a flesh organ. It is the center of the function of the soul—the mind, will, and emotions—and the spirit. This is where our desires and thoughts come forth. When our desire aligns with God's desire for our lives, it affects the progress of our faith.

The thing we need to do is decide what these desires are. Next, we need to look at the reality of desire because our desires reveal who we are. Our desires reveal our character, motivations, purposes, thoughts, and plans. But most of all, these desires disclose the degree of purity in our lives. Being indecisive about our heart's desire is influenced mainly by other people—by what they have, where they have been, and who they have had a relationship with—and we continually change what we desire. Therefore, we need to search for ourselves and decide what we genuinely want out of life. If we honestly don't know the desires of our hearts, how can we ask God to give us our heart's desires? People have said to be careful about what you ask God for. You will be in trouble if you ask the wrong thing, and he gives you the wrong thing. We will never have to worry about God giving us the wrong thing. We need to be careful about manipulating our circumstances, with the enemy helping us receive what we want when it is not what God wants us to have. We do need to ask God what desire is truly in our hearts.

So, what has God promised us in this passage of Scripture? It is what it looks like; it is what it says precisely. It is a divine promise with human responsibility. It is a sacred promise we can bet our lives on. We have the responsibility to delight ourselves in the Lord.

There are two sides to every story regarding delight in the Lord. On one side, you have the church, where it's all about the experience, tears, laughter, dance, and shouts of hallelujah. They believe that the hunger for experiences expresses their delight in the Lord. Of course, these things happen and are valid to some extent, but there has to be a healthy balance. Then you have the more legalistic side, where they believe God only delights in us when we act according to and live up to his expectations, which also has some validity with a healthy balance. God wants us to live in right standing with him, meaning doing what is right in his eyes and living according to his Word and instructions.

To delight ourselves in the Lord is to take pleasure in him. We take pleasure in knowing, talking, praying, worshipping, serving, and being aware of his presence. He is the most delightful person we know. Knowing him brings satisfaction and fulfillment. Therefore, we cannot live half-hearted Christian lives and delight ourselves in the Lord.

He knows we are not perfect—that is where his grace covers us. Grace is God's unmerited favor. We cannot earn it, buy it, or invoke it—it is given to us by the Lord because of his love for us. I am so grateful for his grace because I've learned that he expresses his love to us by his grace. When we fall short, make bad decisions, don't act according to his Word, disobey what he has asked of us, or life beats us up, his grace is always there. The following Scripture would come to mind when I felt abandoned by God and ignored, hurt, or like a failure. Yet God said he would never leave me or forsake me. Hallelujah!

> A broken reed He will not break [off] And a dimly burning wick He will not extinguish [He will not harm those who are weak and suffering]; He will faithfully bring forth justice. (Isaiah 42:3 AMP).

Even though we may have caused our circumstances because of our decisions, he will not cast us aside, meaning we are not outcasts to him, and he has not forgotten us. He will not break off his relationship with us because we made a mistake or a wrong decision. He knows we do not willfully disobey. We may decide not to do what he has asked, but we are constantly tempted not to obey by the influences of Satan, not from our will. Lucifer (Satan) was not tempted to sin. There was no temptation in heaven—he willfully rebelled against God. We are bombarded by many influences that draw us to contradict God's Word and conform to a different standard.

Elisha spent ten years with Elijah. Then, finally, Elisha knew what he desired. After Elijah was taken to heaven, his mantle fell on Elisha. After that, Elisha returned to Jericho and managed fifty-plus student prophets in the School of the Sons of the Prophets. Elisha chose an assistant and understudy named Gehazi. Now Gehazi was an interpreter for Elisha.

In the previous chapter, God used Elisha to help a poor widow and her two sons. Now, a wealthy Shunammite woman helps Elisha, and God reciprocates because of her hospitable actions. The Shunammite woman is one of many unnamed women in the Bible. She is noted as an important, wealthy, well-to-do, prominent, and influential woman of her day. She is a woman of faith. She and her husband developed their faith through relationships and instructions from the Word of God. Here is her story.

> One day Elisha went to the town of Shunem. A wealthy woman lived there, and she urged him to come to her home for a meal. After that, whenever he passed that way, he would stop there for something to eat. She said to her husband, "I am sure this man who stops in from time to time is a holy man of God. Let's build a small room for him on the roof and furnish it with a bed, a table, a chair, and a lamp. Then he will have a place to stay whenever he comes by." One day Elisha returned to Shunem, and he went up to this upper room to rest. He said to his servant Gehazi, "Tell the woman from Shunem I want to speak to her." When she appeared, Elisha said to Gehazi, "Tell her, 'We appreciate the kind concern you have shown us. What can we

do for you? Can we put in a good word for you to the king or to the commander of the army?'" "No," she replied, "my family takes good care of me." Later Elisha asked Gehazi, "What can we do for her?" Gehazi replied, "She doesn't have a son, and her husband is an old man."

"Call her back again," Elisha told him. When the woman returned, Elisha said to her as she stood in the doorway, "Next year at this time you will be holding a son in your arms!" "No, my lord!" she cried. "O man of God, don't deceive me and get my hopes up like that." But sure enough, the woman soon became pregnant. And at that time the following year she had a son, just as Elisha had said.

One day when her child was older, he went out to help his father, who was working with the harvesters. Suddenly he cried out, "My head hurts! My head hurts!" His father said to one of the servants, "Carry him home to his mother." So, the servant took him home, and his mother held him on her lap. But around noontime he died. She carried him up and laid him on the bed of the man of God, then shut the door and left him there.

She sent a message to her husband: "Send one of the servants and a donkey so that I can hurry to the man of God and come right back." "Why go today?" he asked. "It is neither a new moon festival nor a Sabbath." But she said, "It will be all right." So she saddled the donkey and said to the servant, "Hurry! Don't slow down unless I tell you to." As she approached the man of God at Mount Carmel, Elisha saw her in the distance.

He said to Gehazi, "Look, the woman from Shunem is coming. Run out to meet her and ask her, 'Is everything all right with you, your husband, and your child?'" "Yes," the woman told Gehazi, "everything is fine." But when she came to the man of God at the mountain, she fell to the ground before him and caught hold of his feet. Gehazi began to push her away, but the man of God said, "Leave her alone. She is deeply troubled, but the LORD has not told me what it is."

Then she said, "Did I ask you for a son, my lord? And didn't I say, 'Don't deceive me and get my hopes up'?" Then Elisha said to Gehazi, "Get ready to travel; take my staff and go! Don't talk to anyone along the way. Go quickly and lay the staff on the child's face." But the boy's mother said, "As surely as the LORD lives and you yourself live, I won't go home unless you go with me." So Elisha returned with her.

Gehazi hurried on ahead and laid the staff on the child's face, but nothing happened. There was no sign of life. He returned to meet Elisha and told him, "The child is still dead." When Elisha arrived, the child was indeed dead, lying there on the prophet's bed. He went in alone and shut the door behind him and prayed to the LORD. Then he lay down on the child's body, placing his mouth on the child's mouth, his eyes on the child's eyes, and his hands on the child's hands. And as he stretched out on him, the child's body began to grow warm again!

Elisha got up, walked back and forth across the room once, and then stretched himself out again on the child. This time the boy sneezed seven times and opened his eyes! Then Elisha summoned Gehazi. "Call the child's mother!" he said. And when she came in, Elisha said, "Here, take your son!" She fell at his feet and bowed before him, overwhelmed with gratitude. Then she took her son in her arms and carried him downstairs. (2 Kings 4:8–37)

Verses 8–10

One day Elisha went to the town of Shunem. A wealthy woman lived there, and she urged him to come to her home for a meal. After that, whenever he passed that way, he would stop there for something to eat. She said to her husband, "I am sure this man who stops in from time to time is a holy man of God. Let's build a small room for him on the roof and furnish it with a bed, a table, a chair, and a lamp. Then he will have a place to stay whenever he comes by."

In ancient times people traveling depended upon the hospitality of people in the cities as they traveled from place to place. This was especially true of the prophets. We see her Christlike character in her generosity from the heart with sincere motives in providing meals for Elisha when he passed by her home during his travels. She also helped lift the burden by sensing a need to provide a resting place and fellowship for the man of God. We need to be sensitive to the needs of others. In doing this she shows there is no selfishness in her, and she is willing to support the work of the Lord. We need to be responsive and encouraging to the call of God on other people's lives.

Verses 12–13

> He said to his servant Gehazi, "Tell the woman from Shunem I want to speak to her." When she appeared, Elisha said to Gehazi, "Tell her, 'We appreciate the kind concern you have shown us. What can we do for you? Can we put in a good word for you to the king or to the commander of the army?'" "No," she replied, "my family takes good care of me."

When servants of God receive hospitality, they must be ready to give their gifts in return. Therefore, out of gratitude, Elisha was willing to do anything in his power for this woman and her family. This woman shows us that she has no selfishness, self-centeredness, or self-interest. Her motive was to be a blessing to this man of God. She didn't need recognition or anything else.

Verses 16–17

> "Next year at this time you will be holding a son in your arms!" "No, my Lord!" she cried. "O man of God, don't deceive me and get my hopes up like that." But sure enough, the woman soon became pregnant. And at that time the following year she had a son, just as Elisha had said.

In the ancient world, a barren womb was considered a disgrace and a physical defect. The promise spoken by the prophet would address the desire and dream she had buried deep inside, which had now gone dormant. Nevertheless, we can see the pain is still there even after many years. Her statement, "No, my Lord. Don't deceive me and get my hopes up" is a defensive mechanism to protect her from the hurt and pain of not being able to conceive. She may have tried different things, or perhaps she had a miscarriage. She probably dealt with many negative emotions such as guilt, shame, disappointment, and frustration with herself. Perhaps other obstacles stood against the promises of God in her life. At this point, she began to look at the promises of God as a lie. Many of us have had promises of God declared over us, but because we keep encountering one wall after another, we begin to question, "God, did you ever speak to me? Or was this all a lie?"

Elisha discerned that she had a desire for a child. God will not force a blessing on us—there has to be an agreement on earth. Nevertheless, she embraced the word of the Lord by acting on it by having relations with her husband. Her action shows she had faith in God's spoken word. This incredible noblewoman did not allow her past hurts, pain, disappointments, and ridicule to affect her present day and her future. Our past does not need to dictate who we are in our present day or our future. The choice is ours—we can have the mindset of a victim or a victor. She trusted in the word, fulfilling her heart's desire.

On one of my mission trips, I was asked to pray for a couple regarding having children. The doctors told this couple there was nothing medically that could help them. So, after hearing about their situation, the Lord told me to say to them that they would become pregnant. The Lord told me to speak this word to them: "You will conceive twin boys one year from today." God's word is absolute—they delivered twin boys within one day of that year.

The remainder of her story is recorded in verses 18–37.

The woman gave birth to a son, promised by the word of the Lord, and the promise grew into a young man. She and her family, and Elisha, enjoyed several years with the promised blessing. Theologians say he was approximately twelve years old when things changed.

When the Lord brings about the desires of your heart, the enemy will come along and try to kill that dream. The woman's son went to help his father in the harvest field, working in the sweltering heat for a prolonged time. The son exclaimed, "My head! My head!" His father was a wise older man and told his servants to take him to his mother. Why to his mother? Because she had carried him for nine months and then birthed him. When we have held on to a dream for years, no one can care for it except the one who carried it and birthed it.

It was customary in Israel to make inquiries of the prophet at the time of the new moon, which marked the beginning of the month and spiritual renewal, or on the Sabbath, the seventh day of the week, from Friday evening until Saturday evening. These were the times to seek the counsel of the prophet. Her husband asked, but she had hidden the matter from her husband. She did not tell him that this concerned their son; he did not know what was happening. But it was in her wisdom that she hid this matter because she concealed it from anything that would be in opposition to her faith. See, sometimes, when we are experiencing disappointment, it's not the time for us to share with people and engage in what we are experiencing, because what we are doing at that moment is finding agreement in the wrong thing. We must remember that with God all things are possible and not allow God's promise to leave our lives prematurely. So she told her husband, "It will be all right," meaning, "All is well."

The natural thing would be to prepare your child's body for the tomb, but she doesn't do that. When her world collapses, she doesn't run to the bar, engage in wrong activities, stop attending church and reading her Bible, and quit journaling. She doesn't have the prophet's room torn down and sell all the furniture. She didn't do any of this. Instead, she said to herself, "I need to get back to the man of God as fast as possible." She had to travel approximately three hours to reach the man of God. We have a better covenant— we need only two seconds because we have access to God immediately. It makes me wonder what she was thinking during the three hours of travel. Her faith confession was, "It will be all right." The devil must have been trying to convince her that this would be another disappointment and not to go to the man of God. He wanted her to quit and give up, go home, and bury her son. But this woman would not give up until she heard the continuation of God's word regarding these circumstances. God always has a plan for all of life's situations.

Her thoughts and actions reflected her faith, and we must have the same determination to pursue God's Word in every situation. It started with the Word of God and will end with the Word of God. Now Elisha told Gehazi to go and lay his staff on the boy's face, but nothing happened. You can't be in a church that doesn't believe in the whole gospel when you need a breakthrough.

At one of the churches I pastored in California, a man was diagnosed with cancer and treatment wasn't working. He was in a church that didn't believe God still healed. So, a member of our church told him how God had healed people through our ministry. This man came to church, and the Lord told me to pray for him because he would heal him. I told him God wanted me to pray for him, and God would heal him of cancer. So, we obeyed the word of the Lord and prayed for him. He went to the doctors later that week, and the tumor was gone. He was encouraged to attend a church that believed in healing, but he chose to stay in his church that didn't believe in healing, and the cancer returned several months later. He came back for prayer, and the Lord told me to pray but said he was taking this person home to heaven. I asked why. The Lord said he would not stay healed if I healed him again. so, we prayed, but several weeks later he died. So, I would encourage everyone to pray about a church, listen to the Lord, and attend that church.

After Gehazi laid the staff on the boy's face and nothing happened, he met Elisha and the child's mother upon their return. Elisha went upstairs to where the boy was lying. Now Elisha was willing to do whatever the Lord told him, so he stretched out and laid on the boy, eye to eye, mouth to mouth, and hands to hands. The boy's body began to grow warm. The Lord taught me that when you are in unfavorable circumstances or situations, after seeking the Lord, look for minor signs of life, for this is the beginning of the breakthrough. After the boy's body began to grow warm, Elisha turned away and walked back and forth in the room. He stretched out on the boy again, and this time the boy sneezed seven times. Finally, the boy opened his eyes because life came back to him.

The mother came in and showed gratitude to God for what he had done through his servant Elisha. Then she picked up her son and went downstairs. Her future was alive. We need to be grateful for all the Lord has done, strengthening our faith and reliance on God to have the breakthrough during hard circumstances. We will receive direction for our breakthrough as we fellowship and communicate with God.

CHAPTER SIX

Prayer

To understand how important prayer is, we should understand the foundation. First, prayer is a lifestyle and one of the essential kingdom principles that affect what happens on earth. Prayer is not optional for the believer. Most people don't pray because they have misconceptions about prayer. Prayer is the highest priority in the life of the believer, but the enemy tries to hinder and discourage us, and I think therefore so many of God's children don't pray.

Why is prayer so important? Because without God, we can do nothing; without us, God won't do anything on earth. There is a dependency God created between himself and humanity. God designed an arrangement between earth and heaven to make humanity the spiritual authority on earth. God made it a requirement for humanity to give him access to earth through the authority he gave them. God willfully limited himself concerning access to affairs on earth. He made it necessary for us to be the ones who give the legal right for him to interfere on earth. This is found in Genesis 1:26, where God established prayer. God said we, the Holy Trinity, will make man in our likeness—not physical but spiritual and moral equivalence—and let them have complete authority and dominion over the entire earth. Therefore, prayer is not optional—it is necessary because prayer is us giving God access to earth through our faith and our belief.

Have you ever wondered why the Lord puts up with our little quirks, rebellions, and sins? Every human person God has used has flaws. The Bible is a record of weak people. Moses used to curse. He cursed a rock, yet God said, "I have to deal with this guy" because God needs someone to give him access to the affairs of earth. Abraham slept with the maid and had an illegitimate child, but God still used him to bring about a nation. David killed Goliath, then committed adultery with a woman and killed her husband to hide it, but God still used him to be the greatest king. Because God needs us, he tells us, "Please don't sin," not just for our sake but also for his. Psalm 66:18 states that the Lord will not hear my prayers if I regard iniquity in my heart. Our sin can block God's activity on earth. God put us on earth to be his ambassadors.

Jesus stated that the church should be a house of prayer because that is what should take place there the most. So, Jesus made prayer the priority in the corporate gathering. Therefore, what can and cannot take place on earth is connected to corporate and personal prayer.

Prayer is the route to our heavenly Father. Prayer is about our relationship and not about the words we use. When praying, we must be aware not to have divided loyalty to God. We cannot be double-minded. When we communicate with our heavenly Father, we need to be in faith, trusting him to respond and share with us.

> But when you ask him, be sure that your faith is in God alone. Do not waver, for a person with divided loyalty is as unsettled as a wave of the sea that is blown and tossed by the wind. Such people should not expect to receive anything from the Lord. Their

loyalty is divided between God and the
world, and they are unstable in everything
they do. (James 1:6–8)

I am not sure about you, but I have asked why praying
regularly is so hard. It seems we can pray when in need or
when all hell is breaking loose. But when things are going
well, there is no time or desire to pray. My prayers become
ineffective because my mind wanders or is consumed
with other thoughts. As a result, like the disciples, I have
sometimes fallen asleep. Not my finest moments! I have
learned that prayer is a discipline, like playing a sport or a
musical instrument. It takes practice and dedication and
consistency. When done regularly, we begin to flow—it's easy
and not a burden.

So, what is prayer? Prayer is a personal request to God,
who loves and cares about us. It is communication, but
it is not one-sided. It is a dialogue with the Lord because
prayer is relational. The discussion could include thanking,
praising, confessing, or making a request. When fully and
wholeheartedly engaged in, it will encapsulate all of who we
are: spirit, soul (mind, will, and emotions), and body. Prayer
can take place anytime and anywhere.

> Whenever you pray, be sincere and not like
> the pretenders who love the attention they
> receive while praying before others in the
> meetings and on street corners. Believe me,
> they've already received their reward. But
> whenever you pray, go into your innermost
> chamber and be alone with Father God,
> praying to him in secret. And your Father,
> who sees all you do, will reward you openly.
> When you pray, there is no need to repeat
> empty phrases, praying like the Gentiles do,
> for they expect God to hear them because

of their many words. There is no need to imitate them, since your Father already knows what you need before you ask him.

Pray like this: "Our Beloved Father, dwelling in the heavenly realms, may the glory of your name be the center on which our lives turn. Manifest your kingdom realm and cause your every purpose to be fulfilled on earth, just as it is in heaven. We acknowledge you as our Provider of all we need each day. Forgive us the wrongs we have done as we ourselves release forgiveness to those who have wronged us. Rescue us every time we face tribulation and set us free from evil. For you are King who rules with power and glory forever. Amen." (Matthew 6:5–13 TPT)

This Scripture passage has been known as the model prayer, the "how to pray." Jesus here was reflecting on a prayer that Jewish people would recite, the Kaddish, or the mourner's prayer. This prayer model is not a formula or to be repeated verbatim. It's not wrong to come to the Father many times with the same request. The Scripture tells us to ask with persistence. There is freedom when we pray, not a set of rules. We are going to look at different parts of prayer. We will flow in and out of these while praying.

We may start with adoration toward the Father. A father in biblical times was considered a loving person, someone who was reliable, faithful, offered hope, and was a teacher. Our heavenly Father has all those characteristics and more. Adoration is bragging about him for who he is, telling him how good he is, and saying, "You can do all things except fail." Finally, we may use his names and titles: provider, healer, peace, righteousness, King of Kings, Lord of Lords, Alpha and Omega, beginning and the end, author and finisher of our faith.

Then we may flow into confession. I have found that confession has two sides. One side is the confession of sin. According to Psalm 51, confession is a time to refocus our hearts, confess our sins, and ask for help to overcome them. The other side is the confession of faith and belief in Christ. Romans 10 tells us if we will confess that Jesus is Lord, we will be saved. When we confess, this is an acknowledgment and should bring about a change in our behavior. Likewise, admission should bring change if we repent for sin or reveal our belief in our Lord and his Word.

From here, we can flow into thanksgiving, which emphasizes what the Lord has already done and continues to do in our lives. This is our time to confess our gratitude. According to medical research, gratitude has many benefits that affect our minds, wills, and emotions. In essence, we are happier people when we show appreciation.

> Rejoice always and delight in your faith; be unceasing and persistent in prayer; in every situation [no matter what the circumstances] be thankful and continually give thanks to God; for this is the will of God for you in Christ Jesus. (1 Thessalonians 5:16–18 AMP)

From here, we ask something from God. This petition or supplication can be for your need or someone else's. This could also be a time of intercession. We don't have to follow this pattern when we pray. Remember, prayer is communicating or dialoguing with our Father. Jesus taught his disciples how not to pray. He told them that if they didn't have a relationship in their prayer time in secret, they could not think they would publicly accomplish anything.

God looks to the time we spend secretly communicating with him, looking to see that we don't just want something from him but want a personal relationship with him. This communication time brings heaven into the natural realm where we live and operate. The process for this is prayer.

In Luke's account of the lesson on prayer, the disciples ask Jesus to teach them to pray because they have been with him, seeing his power manifested in miracles and the connection between his prayer and the results. They wanted in on these results—we should want the same results. This request to be taught how to pray is what led Jesus to the Lord's Prayer, as it is known. This is a prayer that Jesus could never pray because it says, "Forgive us our sins," and he would never need to ask for forgiveness. So, the lesson is him teaching us how we need to pray.

The prayer is divided into two sections. The first section concerns God—it's about his name, kingdom, and will. The second section is about our daily bread, sins, and temptations. Then the prayer closes with God again: "For yours is the kingdom, the power, and the glory." So, the flow is God—us—God. Prayer is not an informal conversation to inform God. He already knows what we want to talk about. He wants to see whether you wish to speak to him about it.

Just because God knows something doesn't mean he will act on it. He knows of everything, but he will not work on some things until there is relational communication with him about them. His knowledge does not equal his action. God knows what we need, but he wants to see if we want him or just a meeting for a required result. Prayer becomes the answer to that question.

Jesus said to pray this way. This is a guide or framework for praying, and it could be used as an outline for communicating with God. There are several things we need to consider. First, when Jesus stated, "Our Father," he was letting us know we are not an only child. Why did Jesus tell us to approach God as our Father and not just as his Father? If we are parents and one of our children wants to act like our only child, there will be conflict between the other siblings and their father or daddy, who must relate to the whole family equally. So, we can't be in a family of multiple people and function like the only child.

It's *our* Father, and therefore God has said he will not do certain things for one of his children if they are not connected to the rest of the family. So, any unchurched, uninvolved Christian is blocking the Father from answering their personal needs because they don't want to be related to the family. When I was pastoring and counseling, I encountered several individuals who did not want to be connected to God's church—not just my church but any church. They wanted no accountability. They were not open to the opportunity to help other people. I understand the church has hurt people, but before going to a church, we need to pray and ask our Father where to go—there is no perfect church here. We ask so that we can function in whatever form of ministry the father wants us to be a part of. We all have something to contribute that could enrich or change someone's life.

Our Father is a giver, and when he sees us relating to his church family, we receive more from him. If we are fathers, we need to find out what a true healthy father is, so we look to our Father in heaven to see what kind of fathers we are supposed to be. God is a father by position—he cares for his children. In the Bible, the father was head of the household. The Lord said, "I am the God of Abraham, Isaac, and Jacob." He is their Father as well as ours. The Father always made his covenants with the father because the father held the post of responsibility. So, if you are a man, God has you, by position, in the place of responsibility for your home and your children.

In the Bible, it was the father's responsibility to raise the children, not the mothers. So, the Bible tells us in Ephesians 6:4 for the fathers to raise their children. The mother's role is to help fill in the gaps when the father cannot be there. If the father doesn't own this responsibility, he may be a father by title but not by position, because he does not carry the responsibility for raising the children, which belongs in the hands of the man.

What would you do if you were the devil and wanted to destroy the family unit? First, get rid of the fathers from the home because by getting rid of the fathers, you cancel the position, creating an additional burden on the mothers and perhaps damaging the children. So, the devil got the fathers away from the household so that people would have a distorted view of what a true heavenly Father is like. Father is a position to be held, so we need to look at our heavenly Father, who takes responsibility for all his children and all of us who declare Jesus as Lord.

In addition to raising the children, a true father is to provide for and protect his children. God told Adam, "I'm going to make you a provider" before he was head of the household. God provided for him, so he could provide for his family. So, in essence, God is saying, "I'm your Father and want you to be their father." In addition to the position and being the provider was protection. You, Adam, are to guard the garden, and if you protect the garden under me, I will guard you.

If you start with your human father, and your father is not worth following, and you transfer that bad situation to your heavenly Father, you will have a bad attitude toward God. The Lord showed me how this relates to pastoring. I was a pastor by position, but the apostle Paul said (in 1 Timothy) that this role is to gather the congregation. So, I was not just occupying the position, but I was to father the lives of those God has placed under me. I was to care for their well-being because that's what fathers do. Fathers don't just show up to eat; they show up to care. So, our heavenly Father has a position—he is a provider and a protector. This is the Father we talk to when we pray.

Now our Father is in heaven and not on earth. Our Father is a heavenly Father, which is critical because we live on earth, operate by our senses, and are limited by time and space because we are earthbound. The good news is that our heavenly Father does not work by feelings and is not bound as we are to the earth, time, and space. He dwells in heaven.

Daniel 4:26 says heaven rules over the earth, so we need to know that our unseen Father, who operates in heaven, rules over the world when we pray. Therefore, the limitations of our earthly human fathers are not the limitations of our heavenly Father. If we put all our marbles on our earthly fathers with their limits, we will miss out on the power and ability of our heavenly Father, who is not subject to the world.

We should be glad our earthly fathers don't have the last word. If you were raised without a father or with an abusive or neglectful one, I want you to know that earthly fathers don't have the final say over your life, recovery, stability, or provision. Your heavenly Father, who operates out of a different realm and has your best interest in his heart, has you covered.

What can we learn from Jesus when he prayed while on earth? First, when Jesus was on earth, he prayed to God as his Father every time he prayed relationally. So, prayer is a personal relationship with our heavenly Father. Second, I only found that Jesus ever prayed and called the Father "God" when he was on the cross. He said, "My God, why have you forsaken me?" He made that statement because Jesus was covered with our sins on the cross, so there was no fellowship with the Father.

> Jesus cautioned her, "Mary, don't cling to me, for I haven't yet ascended to God, my Father. And he's not only my Father and God, but now he's your Father and your God! Now go to my brothers and tell them what I've told you, that I am ascending to my Father—and your Father, to my God—and your God!" (John 20:17 TPT)

Why would we need to know that? Jesus, who was about to leave, was letting us know this because the same Father that helped him on earth, he has made available to us because we are as much the Father's child as Jesus is. The Bible tells us that Jesus is seated at the right hand of the Father in heaven, and Ephesians 2:6 says, "We are seated with him." So, Jesus is informing us that we have the same level of intimacy based on God's will that the Father had with Jesus. The Father wants to have this intimacy with every one of his children if we will relate to him as Abba Father. Abba is an Aramaic word that means father and is used to express personal intimacy, confidence, trust, and affection.

Unfortunately, some of us have had wrong teaching regarding our heavenly Father. Some of us should pray, "Our judge who is in heaven," because we walk around feeling a hammer over our heads and thinking God is out to get us. Yes, God does have a standard, but within his discipline there is love and gentleness. But that's not the kind of relationship he wants us to pursue. He wants us to seek after an intimate relationship, so we sense and experience his love, not his discipline. We need to grow into this because when we start experiencing him on the Father's level, not the judge's level, we develop intimacy with him personally. What he wants is to speak to his kids. Prayer is his child talking to their father.

Prayer is the key to overcoming. If we struggle with obtaining a breakthrough, prayer provides the strength and power to overcome the struggles and bring a breakthrough. The apostle Paul tells us in Ephesians 6:10–19 to put on the whole armor of God that has been given to us. This armor is used for spiritual warfare and protects us from the enemy. We must be persistent in prayer if we are to overcome, meaning we need to communicate with God constantly. This will keep us in the presence of God. There is power in prayer, and the Holy Spirit is what drives our prayer. The Holy Spirit inspired the written Word of God, and that is who lives in us.

The Holy Spirit knows the intent of our prayers because he dwells in our hearts. So he takes our words, reveals our underlying greatest needs, and presents them perfectly to the Father in heaven (Romans 8:26–27). The Holy Spirit is praying for us, and we gain access to God through our faith. When we pray, the Holy Spirit is involved. Therefore, we address our prayers to the Father, and the Holy Spirit takes them to the Son of God, who is seated at the right hand of the Father, making intercession for believers. Have you noticed that the Holy Trinity is involved every time we pray? The Holy Spirit is in us, Jesus is interceding for us, and the Father is on the throne.

The enemy wants to attack us with distractions, temptations, and doubts so we will not pray. We need to guard our prayer time—one way of doing this is to schedule it. Prioritize your time to pray and keep your prayer flowing daily. We should encourage everything that feeds and fosters our prayer life, focusing our prayer time as we can and getting a plan together for that time. We shouldn't just pray when we feel like it because we won't feel like it as much as we should. What happens then is prayer doesn't get done. Colossians 4:2 tells us to be faithful to prayer and to stay alert and intercede, giving thanks to God. Then as we pray, we will start to align our wills to his, which brings more answers to our prayers. Prayer will require us to persevere through the times we don't feel like praying. We must soldier through and keep going because we are called to pray.

When we pray, we need to focus on God and remove all distractions so that when we talk to God, we can hear his voice or learn how to hear his voice. To focus and stay focused on God and what he is saying, we need to let go of our burdens. It becomes challenging to hear God's voice when we continue to carry our loads, cares, and anxieties. One thing we can do to help leave the burden and allow us to focus is put on some worship music, because worship brings the anointing that breaks the heaviness and help us focus on God. We can also meditate on Scripture. Suppose for some reason, after we enter God's presence and pray, we are still burdened. In that case, this means we never gave the burden to God. First Peter 5:7 tells us to cast, pour, and give all our trouble, care, and anxiety to the Lord, meaning leave it with him, because he passionately cares for us.

The ability to hear God's voice is innate, meaning we're born again with it—it is in our nature and characteristics. When we are born again, we exchange our old nature for God's nature and characteristics. Knowing that we need to learn how to operate in that new nature and character also comes with maturity. Just like a child who has to learn how to speak. A child will say what's on their mind with no filters, but once they understand, they need to mature in their words.

We need to have the desire to hear God's voice. God's voice can be heard when we prepare the atmosphere to receive him in fellowship. He shows up in a prepared atmosphere. We should prepare our hearts and minds to receive from our loving Father. The preparation starts with setting an appointment to meet daily with the Father, at a specific time and place. Remember, a missed appointment will turn into a disappointment. Next, we need to be still by settling our thoughts. Worship is a great way to calm our minds.

What should we pray about? Whatever is on our hearts. Prayer is the transference of a burden, need, desire, or want. In Scripture we are called sheep, and Jesus is the shepherd. However, sheep are not designed to carry burdens—they are not pack animals. Often, this is what we do when we pray: we lay the burden at the Lord's feet, but after prayer, we pick up the burden again and continue to carry it. People have shared their burdens with me and asked me what they should do, and I would advise them to give that burden to God. They would reply, "I have done that many times." So, they had not indeed transferred the burden.

Here is a simple prayer: "Lord, help me to value hearing your voice and make room and time in my life to hear your voice. In Jesus's name, amen."

CHAPTER SEVEN

Pursuing God

We are people in pursuit, and we pursue many different things in our lives—for instance, relationships, wealth, position, and sports, to name a few. So many things. Yet with all these pursuits, I wonder where God fits into our lives. We need to ask ourselves these questions: Is he someone we pursue? What place does he hold in our lives—first, middle, last, just when there is an emergency—or is he an afterthought? Where is God in our lives, from morning until evening? Where is God in our thoughts?

The Lord is a pursuing God. He loves us very much, which is why he is the initiator of our pursuit. In Philippians 2 the apostle Paul states that God is working in us, creating a desire that enables us to be strengthened to please him. In the gospel of John, chapter 6 says that nobody can pursue Jesus until the Father draws, brings, and gives the desire to seek Jesus. But the question is, why would we seek something we already have? According to Psalm 105, we are called to action, to seek more of his strength and help, more of him. We are too deeply and continually long for his presence. Unfortunately, many people are satisfied with a superficial relationship, meaning they don't have a real sense of purpose and direction. It is a casual acquaintance with God. That is not what the Christian life is. It's about living for the Lord, and it is to be taken seriously.

Matthew's gospel chapter 7 (author's paraphrase) tells us that many people will say, "Lord did we not prophesy, convey a message for you, use the authority of your name to cast out demons, and do many miracles?" But the Lord's response is "I never knew you." The Christian life is not about the church or ministry but a personal relationship with God. It's spending time with him, getting to know him, and allowing him to speak and guide our lives.

I think about Hebrews chapter 11, which gives us instructions to seek God with faith, trust, and confidence in our hearts, knowing God helps and rewards those who diligently seek him. If I'm seeking him in my relationship, I must desire to go further and know God more intimately.

We need to understand that God doesn't ever want us to be satisfied in our personal and intimate relationship with him. But there is a sense of satisfaction, such as peace and joy. So here is the paradox: the more satisfied we become with him, the more dissatisfied we become. This dissatisfaction creates more hunger and thirst for God. Matthew chapter 5 tells us that when we seek the righteousness of God, he will fill us, and when we thirst and hunger for God, actively seeking him, our relationship deepens. See, God is fathomless. We will never know the fullness of who he is, but he wants us to pursue him from the moment we accept him as our Lord and Savior. To seek him is to pray to him, listen to him, talk to him, and grow with him.

We must keep the fire of our desire hot to know God, which requires discipline. So, desire and discipline work together. We must set our minds, wills, and emotions on pursuing our relationship with God. But we must also understand that we cannot be living a lifestyle of sin over here and seeking God over there. That doesn't work, for either we are going to live a lifestyle of sin, or we are going to seek the Lord. Yes, there are times in our lives when our weaknesses show up as we are seeking and pursuing God. But we have an assurance that as we continue to seek him, he will help us overcome our weaknesses.

The pursuit of God is a one-on-one relationship—an individual and personal seeking of the presence of God. This relationship is a two-way pursuit. There is no formula for the quest. Instead, we must find the best rhythm as we seek him. Some people may have a set time in the morning or the evening. But we need daily fellowship with God, time in his Word, and prayer. This time helps us develop our relationship, strengthening our trust and confidence in his ability to help and guide us in the affairs of life. This relationship is all-inclusive. We must realize that the result of pursuing God is a progressive revelation, and one of the keys to seeking God is to have an expectation. We should live in a place of anticipation that we will experience God as we pursue him. The expectation is not a feeling but is based on our faith in him and his Word.

The Beginning of the Presence

To completely understand his presence, which is what we seek and pursue, we need to start where it began in the garden of Eden. The Genesis account starts with the Creator, who is powerful, brilliant, and creative. He loves beauty and order and is perfect. So out of this love, he creates a universe, plants a garden, and then forms humanity for several reasons. First, we were created in his likeness, which is what transformation is all about—being restored to his image. He gave us to have authority over all of creation for him, so we were ultimately created to walk in a personal relationship with him. Before the fall, man and woman walked daily in the garden with God. This is how the presence started, but humanity lost sight due to the great rebellion, so the daily intimacy with God ended. What happened next was humanity was expelled from the garden. So they were, in a sense, out there on their own. But God, who removed them, also loved them very much, and he would continue to pursue them from that point on, restoring their presence.

After the expelling from the garden, chaos and disorder entered the earth as sin and death spread to every part of humanity. We see it recorded in the time of Noah with the flooding of the land, and then there was the Tower of Babel. So it continued until the turning point with a man who grew up in Ur of the Chaldeans (modern-day Iraq), a pagan culture where the people worshipped Nanna, the moon god. His name was Abram. So, God revealed himself to Abram, and he said to him, "Come and follow me." Abram said yes, left his country and family, and pursued God. But God told Abram he would bless him and make him a great nation, and the entire world would be blessed one day. So, five to seven hundred years later, God kept that promise, and the family of Abraham became the nation of Israel.

There were two to three million Israeli people in Egypt, and they had become enslaved. So, God raised Moses to be the instrument God would use to release them from captivity. God set them free, and they traveled and came to Mount Sinai, also known as Mount Horeb, and the children of Israel entered a relationship with God. In Exodus 33, starting in verse twelve, God told Moses that his presence would go with him. Here again, this confirms that we were created to live in the presence of God.

When we spend time with the Lord, we need to be aware of the company we are entering into. So don't just say a few quick prayers, read off your list, say amen, and call it a day. We are entering into the holy presence of God. This time is for him; what does he want to say in our time together? We should desire to have the presence around us, with us, in us, and guiding us—this should be a priority.

God's Pursuit of Us

Up to this point, we have seen God pursuing us, first through a man named Abram, then through a nation, and now the next step is in a tent. God saw that his children lived in tents, so he would live in a tent because we were in a married relationship. The Lord wanted to come live with us, so he instructed what kind of tent it would be, a unique dwelling with specific features. This tent would have certain dimensions and symbolism to give understanding and remind his children of their relationship with God.

So, God instructed them to make him a sanctuary where he could dwell, live, reside, and abide among them in fellowship. This sanctuary was known by different names—tabernacle and tent of meeting. This tent is where the Lord would meet with his children. God was entering into a covenant with his people. He was unequivocal, not just about the tent but the placement of it. His instruction was to place the tent in the center of the nation. This placement indicates that God wants to be in the center of our lives. After the sanctuary was completed, God came and dwelt with his children, and his presence brought the cloud of glory. This is the point when God's presence returned to the earth. For the first time since the garden, God's presence had returned, and from this point on, the cloud of glory would direct the nation. When the cloud moved, God's people moved; when the cloud stayed, the nation stayed. This scenario is a beautiful picture of how the Lord wants to direct our lives.

When God moves, we move. When God stands still, we wait, listen, and follow.

Now let's jump ahead four hundred years. The people of God moved into the land and conquered it. King David was on the throne and had built a beautiful palace. Next, his son Solomon would construct a wonderful temple. The construction of this temple took seven years, and then it was dedicated to the Lord, asking him to dwell with his people. God said yes, and the glory of the Lord came, but this was not the end of the story. From this point on, the temple for the Jewish people became the holiest place in the world. The temple was the place where heaven meets earth.

We will examine the story of the Samaritan woman's dialogue with Jesus at the well. This encounter is recorded in the gospel of John chapter 4. In this conversation, the woman asked Jesus this question: where would she go to meet the presence of God? The Jewish people said the temple was in Jerusalem, but the Samaritans had built an alternative temple at Mount Gerizim. Jesus's reply is critical: there was a time coming, that now was here, when everything would change. God is not only going to live in a temple.

After the temple was constructed in the Old Testament, starting with King David and then the prophets, God began prophesying that one day he would come even closer to his children. He wasn't going to live in a temple made of human hands, but he was going to live in a person. This was when prophecies started being spoken about the son coming from King David's line. So many things were said about this son, like his coming from eternity, and that his name would be called wonderful counselor, prince of peace, mighty God. So, what transpired was a mysterious unfolding of a son of the line of David, which was God coming in this son, but in a way that wasn't clear. Then, after Jesus came, it all became clear.

So, the King of Kings was born, and his name was to be called Emmanuel, meaning God is with us. The apostle John in chapter 1 starts to fill us in on the backstory of Genesis chapter 1. John states that the Lord will dwell with us, and we will see his glory. Still, God wants to come closer to his children. God himself became flesh and dwelt among us, but he planned for more. From this point, we must return to the conversation with the Samaritan woman at the well.

Jesus said the time is now that we will not need a building to experience the presence of God. God is a spirit, not a physical being, and God is looking for people who will worship him in spirit and truth. A new day is coming. Jesus lived, died, and rose from the dead. His death and resurrection made atonement for sin once and for all for humanity.

We were expelled from the garden because we couldn't live in the presence of God with sin in us. There was a veil in the tabernacle because you can't enter God's presence with sin. But when Jesus died, the veil was torn from top to bottom. Why was the veil torn? Because sin had been atoned for, and God was returning to his people. Now this paved the way for us to become the temple of God. Once the veil was removed, we could fulfill what we were created for, to glorify God and enjoy him forever.

In the New Testament, we are told that our bodies are the temple of God. They are where the Holy Spirit comes to reside. But often we are undersold and lack understanding regarding our bodies as the temple of God. Therefore, we have taken this to simply mean stop drinking and smoking. Unfortunately, we miss the bigger picture and thus miss the bigger plan God has for us.

The preceding is an epic story, and we have been called to live epic lives. There was a time when God invaded the tabernacle, and there was a time when he abided in the temple. There was a time when God came in the flesh, and there was a time when God came into us. If we are followers of Jesus, our sin has been atoned for, and the presence of God has returned. The Spirit of God is upon us and within us, so we become the place where heaven meets earth. We are the temple of God, individually and corporately as the body of Christ. Either way, we are the temple where God dwells, abides, and takes up residence. Wherever we go, the presence of God goes.

The apostle Paul says in 2 Corinthians 3:17 that where the Holy Spirit of God is, there the Lord is, and we have freedom, liberty, and emancipation from bondage. In Scripture, sexual immorality is a very big deal. The apostle Paul says that a one-flesh union occurs when you have sex with someone. This union is also known as a soul tie. When people come into our lives, they impact every area of life, and the physical connection or bond is the strongest. So when we come to Jesus, there's a one-spirit union. The Holy Spirit comes to our spirit, making us the temple of God. When sex outside of marriage occurs, the temple of God and the Holy Spirit are now joined to that situation. That is why the Lord says we need to flee and run away from sexual immorality, because we need to glorify God with our temple.

We were created for something more. God's vision is more and higher—he is calling us to something greater. So, we shouldn't allow our temples to be misused sexually.

How will this epic story of God, who restored his presence, end? The events that started in the garden with us walking in the presence of God will end with us dwelling with our Creator, our God and Father, forever in a new city.

> Then I saw a new heaven and a new earth,
> for the old heaven and the old earth had
> disappeared. And the sea was also gone.
> And I saw the holy city, the new Jerusalem,
> coming down from God out of heaven like

> a bride beautifully dressed for her husband. I heard a loud shout from the throne, saying, "Look, God's home is now among his people! He will live with them, and they will be his people. God himself will be with them." (Revelation 21:1–3)

The new city was prepared as a bride, so we can't have any other gods. God is not looking for a one-night stand. He's looking for a lifelong eternal relationship, having eyes for you only. This relationship is about him being our first love, most profound passion, and highest priority, and this is the relationship God is looking for. He is looking for a marriage relationship with us—this has been his vision since day one in the garden. As we can see, God has relentlessly pursued us throughout history, one step at a time. God is looking for people who want to enter this marriage-like relationship. This relationship will not happen for us automatically because we go to church or study—these things are means to an end.

The reason this relationship happens is that we choose to pursue him with our whole hearts. So how do we pursue the presence of God? First, we know we have been created to live in the presence of God. He is our source of life, just like water is to a fish. Something broke when humanity rebelled against God, and now there is a solid dislike for God within society. Because we as a society are broken, we try to meet this need for God with something else, like a person, place, things, or even religious systems. These pursuits for attempting to complete this deep need for God lead only to more brokenness and emptiness. They are worthless pursuits that lead to the loss of God and us.

According to Jeremiah 2:2,5, and 13, when we pursue things other than God, we become like those things, and in the process of pursuing them, we lose touch with our identity in Christ. But on the other hand, if we seek God, the living water, he promises to refresh us with himself. See, living water is water that is continuous and moving. So, God is saying he is our source of life. If we want to know how people respond to God, we need to look at Israel, for they are a case study in responding to God.

How would a person respond when given the advantages of God, the correct teaching and life path? These people turn to pursue creation instead of the Creator. Some seek people, and this can be done in different ways. One way is romance, and we are convinced that if we find the right person and fall in love, this will satisfy our deep longing for God. So, we decide that this person is who we will live for, and we encompass our lives around this relationship. It could be getting married, so we can have children and build our lives around the kids. Then they become the most valued, and we serve and pursue them most in life. Again, we believe that if we make a strong relationship with them, this will satisfy our deep need for God. I have experienced that children love you, and you have a bond with them, but they eventually leave and go about their lives. You can have a close relationship, but it will never replace your deep desire for God. For other people, it is family, and there's nothing better than family. This becomes their top value. For some, it is a form of community, so people become their highest priority. They are hoping their deep need for God will be met.

Some of us will pursue possessions, and we are convinced that the one with the most toys will win. We have bought into the lie that possessions, things that money can buy like security and an extensive portfolio, will cause us to be happy and feel fulfilled. We are trying to fill the gap where God should be.

For others, it is about obtaining a particular position or authority. For example, "If only I could make that team and become the quarterback," or "If I could get into the college of my dreams, I would get the career of my choice. Then I could go up the corporate ladder or get to the corner office." So, there is some pursuit, and you can see this is the highest value in their life. They are willing to sacrifice pretty much anything for it. They may say their family is their priority, but when you look at their life, it doesn't stand out. Because when it comes to family or achievement, the achievement will always win out.

Some people will pursue pleasure, which can come in different varieties or levels of satisfaction. On the lower level would be things like sex, drugs, alcohol, and the party life. This level feeds the senses. On the other side are the slightly more sophisticated people who want to know everything about wines and food, the fine things in life, the suitable perfumes and clothing. These things bring some pleasure.

You can tell who a person's god is by what they pursue the most. What we seek is our highest value, which by definition is our god. So, God is saying through Jeremiah that when we pursue something other than God to satisfy the most profound need of our hearts, it does not fully help. It only temporarily satisfies. The irony is that these things we pursue are good most of the time. People are one of our greatest gifts. Family, friends, spouses, children, and grandchildren are some of the most incredible things in life. If we look at possessions, the Scripture tells us that God richly blesses us with everything to enjoy. Everything he gives is a gift of his love. The pleasures of life are gifts. Satan does not create pleasure—he perverts pleasure. God is the source of all pleasure, and it was his idea. However, it becomes bad when we take a good thing and place it above God. For some reason, we can't learn this within our humanity. If one pursuit doesn't do it, we try another because the fallen nature is wired this way. We all have had some experience with this.

God is still pursuing us, but this time he will not write his laws on tablets of stone but on our hearts. He says he will change us from the inside out to have the capacity for committed love and a real relationship. God tells us according to his Word that he will be our God, and we will be his people.

The Holy Spirit is reshaping us. He has provided everything we need to pursue after God. So when the Holy Spirit is stirring us, we need to respond. But first, we must be intentional about the plan of seeking God. To keep us on track, I suggest starting journaling and writing down the program and goals. What will it look like to follow the plan? What would it look like to not follow the plan? If we journal, we can refer to it as we are in pursuit.

To pursue God, we need wisdom. There is nothing more valuable than wisdom. The knowledge of God is so critical to our lives that Solomon told us that whatever it costs us, it is worth the investment. Solomon wrote in Proverbs 3 that the person who finds wisdom is joyful, which is more profitable than any commodity could ever bring. Understanding brings long life, riches, and honor, and it brings life to those who grab hold of it. Unfortunately, we do not have time to gain knowledge when we live at high speed. We need to learn to slow down. It's okay to say no to other things, so we can obtain the wisdom, knowledge, and direction from God we need. We need to prioritize our time, and what is most valuable to us comes into play.

We need to be renewed. Life is hard, and we get worn down. We become discouraged, so we need to be filled up— we need his strength. To be transformed in our lives, we need his wisdom, and no transformation happens without his knowledge. Wisdom can't be obtained anywhere else but the Word and the Holy Spirit working together, bringing life into our souls. We need his wisdom, discipline, and correction. If we don't have time alone with God, we will not have these things in our lives.

So, we should pursue God at all costs because God spared no expense to pursue us. The rewards are not only eternal but also beneficial in the affairs of our lives today.